LI CH'ING-CHAO:
COMPLETE POEMS

BOOKS BY KENNETH REXROTH

POEMS

The Collected Shorter Poems
The Collected Longer Poems
Sky Sea Birds Trees Earth House Beasts Flowers
New Poems
The Phoenix and the Tortoise
The Morning Star

PLAYS

Beyond the Mountains

CRITICISM & ESSAYS

The Alternative Society
American Poetry in the Twentieth Century
Assays
Bird in the Bush
The Classics Revisited
Communalism, from the Neolithic to 1900
The Elastic Retort
With Eye and Ear

TRANSLATIONS

100 Poems from the Chinese
100 More Poems from the Chinese: Love and the Turning Year
The Burning Heart: Women Poets of Japan
(*with Ikuko Atsumi*)
The Orchid Boat: The Women Poets of China
(*with Ling Chung*)
100 French Poems
Poems from the Greek Anthology
100 Poems from the Japanese
100 More Poems from the Japanese
30 Spanish Poems of Love and Exile
Selected Poems of Pierre Reverdy
Li Ch'ing-chao: Complete Poems (*with Ling Chung*)

AUTOBIOGRAPHY

An Autobiographical Novel

EDITOR

An Anthology of Pre-literate Poetry
The Continuum Poetry Series

李清照

鍾玲 書譯

王紅公

LI CH'ING-CHAO:
COMPLETE POEMS

Translated and edited by
KENNETH REXROTH
and
LING CHUNG

A NEW DIRECTIONS BOOK

Manufactured in the United States of America
First published clothbound and as
New Directions Paperbook 492 in 1979
Published simultaneously in Canada by
George J. McLeod, Ltd., Toronto

Library of Congress Cataloging in Publication Data
Li, Ch'ing-chao, 1081-ca. 1141.
Li Ch'ing-chao, complete poems.
(A New Directions Book)
1. Li, Ch'ing-chao, 1081-ca. 1141. 2. Poets,
Chinese—Biography. I. Rexroth, Kenneth, 1905–
II. Chung, Ling, 1945– III. Title.
PL2682.A27   895.1′1′4   79-15596
ISBN 0-8112-0744-7
ISBN 0-8112-0745-5 pbk.

Cover painting of Li Ch'ing-chao, 11th century, with calligraphy
by Chu Kuang-fu; design by Susan Shapiro

New Directions Books are published for James Laughlin
by New Directions Publishing Corporation,
80 Eighth Avenue, New York 10011

CONTENTS

YOUTH

JOY OF WINE

TO THE TUNE "A DREAM SONG"

I remember in Hsi T'ing
All the many times
We got lost in the sunset,
Happy with wine,
And could not find our way back.
When the evening came,
Exhausted with pleasure,
We turned our boat.
By mistake we found ourselves even deeper
In the clusters of lotus blossoms,
And startled the gulls and egrets
From the sand bars.
They crowded into the air
And hastily flapped away
To the opposite shore.

SPRING ENDS

TO THE TUNE "A DREAM SONG"

Last night fine rain, gusts of wind,
Deep sleep could not dissolve the leftover wine.
I asked my maid as she rolled up the curtains,
"Are the begonias still the same?"
"Don't you know it is time
For the green to grow fat and the red to grow thin?"

THOUGHTS FROM THE WOMEN'S QUARTER

TO THE TUNE "THE SILK WASHING BROOK"

She smiles as she pushes aside
The curtain embroidered with water lilies,
And leans her perfumed cheek
Against the precious duck incense burner.
She gently rolls her eyes as he begs her
To tell him what she is thinking about.

After he has gone,
Her flirtatious face becomes pensive
And radiates the essence of beauty.
She fills half a page
With endearing reproaches,
And sends him her most intimate thoughts.
She makes an assignation,
"Come to me again when the moon
Moves the flower shadows."

ATTRIBUTED TO LI CH'ING-CHAO

TO A SHORT VERSION OF "THE MAGNOLIA FLOWER"

I bought a spray of Spring in bloom
From a flower carrying pole.
It is covered with tiny teardrops
That still reflect the pink clouds of dawn
And traces of morning dew.
Lest my lover should think
The flowers are lovelier than my face
I pin it slanting in my thick black hair
And ask him to compare us.

ATTRIBUTED TO LI CH'ING-CHAO

TO THE TUNE "PICKING MULBERRIES"

It is turning dark,
Sudden wind and rain
Wash away the blazing sunlight.
I play the mouth organ for awhile,
And then lightly powder myself
Before the water-flower ornamented mirror.
In my transparent purple silk nightgown
My white skin glows,
Fragrant and smooth as snow.
I smile to my love and say,
"Tonight within the gauze curtains
Our pillows and mats will be cool."

ATTRIBUTED TO LI CH'ING-CHAO

6

TWO SPRINGS

TO THE TUNE "SMALL HILLS"

Spring has come to the women's quarter.
Once more the new grass is kingfisher green.
The cracked red buds of plum blossoms
Are still unopened little balls.
Blue-green clouds carve jade dragons.
The jade powder becomes fine dust.
I try to hold on to my morning dream.
I have already drained and broken
The cup of Spring.
Flower shadows lie heavy
On the garden gate.
In the orange twilight
Pale moonlight spreads
On the translucent curtain.
Three times in two years
My lord has gone away to the East.
Today he returns,
And my joy is already
Greater than the Spring.

7

RED PLUM BLOSSOMS

TO THE TUNE "SPRING IN THE JADE TOWER"

You permit your red crisp blossoms
To be broken like pieces of jasper.
I visit the southern branches
To see if all the buds have bloomed.
I don't know how long you have refined this perfume,
But I see it encloses and hides a limitless love.
This Taoist priestess withers
Inside a window in Spring,
So depressed and injured by sorrow
She does not even go out on the balcony.
Since the blossoms invited her
To share a little wine she will come.
Who knows, tomorrow morning
The wind may blow them away.

PLUM BLOSSOMS

TO THE TUNE "THE HONOR OF A FISHERMAN"

Already, out of the snow,
You bring news that Spring is here,
Cold plum blossoms, adorning
The glossy jasper branches,
Perfumed faces half showing,
Gracefully fluttering in the middle of the courtyard.
I come, my jade body fresh from the bath,
Newly powdered and rouged.
Even Heaven shares our joy,
Making the bright moon shine splendid on your curving
    flesh.
Let us celebrate with thick green wine in gold cups.
I will not refuse to get drunk
For this flower cannot be compared to other flowers.

WHEN THE PLUMS
BY THE BACK PAVILION BLOOMED
TO THE TUNE "AN IDLE, LOVELY WOMAN"

Frail as thin jade, perfume thick as sandalwood
Deep in the still melting snow—
This year I hate to visit the late blooming plums.

He is in the South in the second story of an inn by the
     river.
Clouds and mist stretch far over the water.

I am here, in the long clear weather
Leaning against the balustrade
With the kingfisher-green curtain rolled low.

A guest comes. We fill our wine cups
And sing together. Here too the water flows into the
     clouds.
We should cut the sunlit branches of blossoms
And not wait until the Tatar flute
Sounds from the West Tower.

PEONIES

TO THE TUNE "I CELEBRATE THE CLEAR SLOW DAWN"

You open the low curtains of the women's quarter in the
    palace.
And carefully the carved railings guard you.
You stand alone in the middle of the balcony in the end
    of Spring.
Your flowerlike face is clear and bright as flowing water.
Gentle, modest, your natural innocence is apparent to all.
All flowers have withered except you.
In the morning breeze, in glittering dew,
You make your morning toilet
And become still more splendid and bewitching.
The wind envies you as you laugh at the moon.
The God of Spring falls in love with you forever.
Over the east side of the city the sun rises
And shines on the ponds and the gardens
And teahouses of the courtesans in the south side.
The perfumed carriages run home.
The banquet tables are cleared of scattered flowers and
    silks.
Who will succeed you when you have become perfumed
    dust?
The Palace of Brilliant Light was not more beautiful,
As the sun rises through the branches of your blossoms.
I pledge my love to you in a gold cup.
As the painted candles gutter and die,
I for one do not welcome the yellow twilight.

WATCHING LOTUSES

TO THE TUNE "GRIEVANCE AGAINST MY YOUNG LORD"

Wind comes on the lake.
The waves spread far and wide.
Already Autumn is ending.
The red lotus blossoms are few,
Their fragrance is sparse.
All men love the reflection in the water
Of the colored mountains
And never stop talking of their beauty.
The lotus pods are ripe.
The lotus leaves have turned old.
Duckweed and rushes are soaked with crystal dew.
Gulls and egrets along the bank
Have their heads tucked beneath their wings,
Or turn their heads away,
As if they too regret
That you must go back so soon.

CASSIA FLOWERS

TO THE TUNE "PARTRIDGE SKY"

Yellow bodies, light in color and weight,
Gentle and soft in character,
Aloof, dispassionate,
Only their perfume is available.
They do not need bright green and red.
They are naturally the first choice of flowers.
The plum blossoms are jealous,
The chrysanthemums embarrassed.
In any exhibition of flowers
They are the queens of mid-Autumn.
Other poets have been without taste
That they never wrote of them in the past.

NINTH DAY, NINTH MONTH
TO THE TUNE "DRUNK WITH FLOWER SHADOWS"

Thin fog under thick clouds,
Sadness endures through the long day.
Auspicious Dragon incense
Rises from the gold animal.
Again it is the Ninth of the Ninth Month.
At midnight my jeweled pillow
And gauze-curtained bed
Were saturated with chill.
Now in the yellow twilight
I drink by the Eastern wall,
And a mysterious perfume fills my sleeves,
And carries away my soul.
The West Wind blows the curtains
And I am frailer than the yellow chrysanthemums.

THE BEAUTY OF WHITE CHRYSANTHEMUMS
TO THE TUNE "BEAUTIES"

It is cold in my small pavilion.
All night my bed curtains sag with damp.
I hate the *hsiao hsiao* of the implacable wind and rain
That twists and breaks your jade flesh.
Your face is not like Yang Kuei-fei flushed with wine,
Nor like Sun Shou's worried brow.
You should not be compared to Chia Wu
Who stole the imperial incense for her lover,
Nor with the lewd Lady Hsü
Who powdered only half her face
To make fun of her one-eyed husband, the Emperor.
These comparisons are not apt.
After careful consideration,
I think your charm is that
Of the poets Ch'ü Yüan and T'ao Ch'ien.
In the breeze your perfume is as
Subtle as the odor of blackberry blossoms.
In the slow end of autumn
You are white as the coming snow,
And frail as transparent jade.
Leaning, leaning toward people with
Congealed sorrow, like the ghost on the shore of the Han
    River,
Who gave her lover a jade pendant and vanished,
Or like the tears of the imperial concubine Lady Pan
Who wrote a poem on a silk fan after she was deserted.

Clear, bright moon, pure wind, changes to thick mist,
    dark rain.
Heaven ordains you will wither
And your faint fragrance disappear.
No matter how much I love you
You will fade but be remembered in this poem.
You will not need to envy
The orchids gathered along the river bank by Ch'ü Yüan
Or the chrysanthemums planted against the east hedge
    by T'ao Ch'ien.

LONELINESS

寂

REMORSE

TO THE TUNE "ROUGED LIPS"

Deep in the silent inner room
Every fiber of my soft heart
Turns to a thousand strands of sorrow.
I loved the Spring,
But the Spring is gone
As rain hastens the falling petals.
I lean on the balustrade,
Moving from one end to the other.
My emotions are still disordered.
Where is he?
Withered grass stretches to the horizon
And hides from sight
Any road by which he might return.

TO THE TUNE "THE SILK WASHING BROOK"

I cannot permit myself
To give way to too many cups of thick amber wine,
Or I will become so drunk
I will lose control of myself.
The first scattered bells
Are borne on the evening breeze.
Auspicious Dragon incense fades
Like my interrupted dream.
The delicate gold-bird hairpins
Fall from my tangled hair.
I awake
In the empty night
Face to face with a
Guttering red candle.

ON SPRING

TO THE TUNE "THE SILK WASHING BROOK"

I idle at the window
In the small garden.
The Spring colors are bright.
Inside, the curtains have not been raised
And the room is deep in shadow.
In my high chamber
I silently play my jade zither.
Far-off mountain caves spit clouds,
Hastening the coming of dusk.
A light breeze brings puffs of rain
And casts moving shadows on the ground.
I am afraid I cannot keep
The pear blossoms from withering.

SPRING IN THE WOMEN'S QUARTER

TO THE TUNE "BEAUTIFUL NIEN NU"

The courtyard is desolate and bleak.
The wind blows the fine rain into slanting lines.
The outer wooden shutters should all be closed.
I love the pussy willows and the returning orioles.
It will soon be the Day of Cold Food,
But the changing weather is still unpleasant.
Supporting my head on my hand,
Somber from too much wine,
I have finished a poem with difficult rhymes.
Now I have nothing to do.
The rows of wild geese are gone from the sky.
They could never carry all my thoughts to him.

For the last few days
The chill has filled my upper rooms.
The screens are unrolled on every side.
Idly I lean on the balustrade.
My quilts were cold, the incense dissipated
And my dreams interrupted.
I was forced to get up
And face my unending sorrow.
The morning dew drips from the young wu-t'ung leaves.
I can still enjoy the beauty of Spring.
The fog lifts and the clouds soar high.
I hope we will have a clear day.

THE DAY OF COLD FOOD

TO THE TUNE "THE SILK WASHING BROOK"

Clear and radiant is the splendor
Of Spring on the Day of Cold Food.
The dying smoke of aloes wood incense
Floats above the jade burner.
My dream is broken, and hidden
Like my flower hair ornaments
Buried in a pile of cushions.
The swallows have not come back
From the Eastern Sea, but already
People are gathering wild flowers and herbs
In the meadow. The plum blossoms by
The river are gone. Catkins
Appear on the willow branches.
And then—in the orange twilight—
Fall widely spaced drops of rain.

23

THOUGHTS FROM THE WOMEN'S QUARTER

TO THE TUNE "THE SILK WASHING BROOK"

Lazy with Spring sickness,
I do not comb my hair
Until the plum blossoms fall
In the courtyard in the evening breeze.
Light clouds drift across and dim the moon.
From the jade duck incense burner
Auspicious Dragon incense rises idly.
The scarlet net tassels droop on the bed.
I eat melon seeds.
I drink the tepid wine left over
In the rhinoceros horn cups.
I try to keep warm
Like the gold tree of the South.

The cries of returning wild geese
Are stilled as the strands of the cloud
Turn blue-green.
Snow falls outside the windows
Of the women's quarters.
The incense smoke rises straight up.
My phoenix hairpins glitter in the candlelight.
A tiny gold pendant in the shape of a lady
Swings under the beak of the phoenix.

Bugles sound. Dawn comes. Drums beat the watch.
The stars in the River of Heaven pale in the dawn.
I long for the Spring
And search for the first flowers,
But the West Wind is still as cold as ever.

25

The wind has stilled.
The fallen petals lie deep
Outside my curtains
Like piles of red snow.
I always remember
When the begonia petals have fallen
That the time has come to mourn for Spring.
The wine drinkers are gone.
The songs are sung.
The jade cups are empty.
The bright lights of the blue-green lamps
Have burned out.
This trance of dark melancholy
Is unbearable,
And unbearable the crying of the nightjars.

SORROW OF DEPARTURE

TO THE TUNE "CUTTING A FLOWERING PLUM BRANCH"

Red lotus incense fades on
The jeweled curtain. Autumn
Comes again. Gently I open
My silk dress and float alone
On the orchid boat. Who can
Take a letter beyond the clouds?
Only the wild geese come back
And write their ideograms
On the sky under the full
Moon that floods the West Chamber.
Flowers, after their kind, flutter
And scatter. Water after
Its nature, when spilt, at last
Gathers again in one place.
Creatures of the same species
Long for each other. But we
Are far apart and I have
Grown learned in sorrow.
Nothing can make it dissolve
And go away. One moment,
It is on my eyebrows.
The next, it weighs on my heart.

FAREWELL LETTER TO MY SISTER
SENT FROM AN INN AT LO CH'ANG
TO THE TUNE "BUTTERFLIES LOVE FLOWERS"

I wipe away my tears
And stain my silk sleeves with rouge and powder.
Over and over I sing the four verses
Of "Sunlight on the Pass."
You said we would be separated
By endless mountains and waters.
Hsiao! Hsiao! I listen to the fine rain
All alone in a lonely inn.
My heart was so troubled at our separation
That I forgot to give you a parting cup for the journey.
So I send you this letter by the wild geese.
At least Shantung Province is not
A far-off island in the Eastern Sea.

The sky turns,
The Autumn light turns,
And my heart aches.
I visit the golden flowers
And realize that the Ninth Day of the Ninth Month
Will soon be here.
I try on a new dress
And taste the new green thick wine.
By turns the weather is windy, rainy, and chilly.
As the orange twilight fills the courtyard
I am overwhelmed with anxiety.
The wine awakens all the sorrow of the past in my breast.
How can I bear the endless night,
The full moon's light on our empty bed,
The sound of the fullers' mallets,
Beating cloth for winter,
The shrill crying of the crickets,
And the lingering notes of the bugles?

THOUGHTS FROM THE WOMEN'S QUARTER

TO THE TUNE
"NOSTALGIA OF THE FLUTE ON THE PHOENIX TERRACE"

The incense is cold in the gold lion.
My quilts are tumbled like red waves.
I get up lazily.
Not yet myself, I comb my hair.
My toilet table is unopened.
I leave the curtains down until
The sun shines over the curtain rings.
I am afraid of this idleness
Which permits dark sorrow to overcome me.
There are so many things I would like to write
But I let them go.
I have become thinner this year
Not due to sickness, not to wine,
Not to the sorrows of Autumn.
Finished. Finished.
This time he is gone for good.
If I sang *The Sunlight in the Pass*
Ten thousand times
I could not hold him.
I think of him far-off at Wu-ling Springs.
Alone in my Ch'in pavilion,
Locked in by fog,
Only the green flowing water
In front of the pavilion
Knows my eyes that stare and stare,
Where new layers of sorrows pile up.

30

AUTUMN LOVE

"A WEARY SONG TO A SLOW SAD TUNE"

Search. Search. Seek. Seek.
Cold. Cold. Clear. Clear.
Sorrow. Sorrow. Pain. Pain.
Hot flashes. Sudden chills.
Stabbing pains. Slow agonies.
I can find no peace.
I drink two cups, then three bowls
Of clear wine until I can't
Stand up against a gust of wind.
Wild geese fly overhead.
They wrench my heart.
They were our friends in the old days.
Gold chrysanthemums litter
The ground, pile up, faded, dead.
This season I could not bear
To pick them. All alone,
Motionless at my window,
I watch the gathering shadows.
Fine rain sifts through the wu-t'ung trees.
And drips, drop by drop, through the dusk.
What can I ever do now?
How can I drive off this word—
Hopelessness?

SPRING ENDS, I

TO THE TUNE "A COMPLAINT TO MY YOUNG LORD"

My dream was broken by the light sound of the water
  clock.
I am sad, upset by last night's thick wine.
My pillow, inlaid with precious stones, has grown cold.
I open the emerald-green panels and face another dawn.
Who swept away the withered red petals from outside
  my door?
Or was it last night's wind?

I no longer hear his jade flute. Where did he go?
The Spring too has departed.
Hard of heart, he has not kept his word to return.
This passion, this remorse,
This time I will ask the moving clouds to seek my lord
  in the East.

ATTRIBUTED TO LI CH'ING-CHAO

SPRING ENDS, II

TO THE TUNE "A COMPLAINT TO MY YOUNG LORD"

Spring is over in the Imperial City.
Behind many doors, in my secluded garden
The grass is green in front of the staircase.

The wild geese have vanished from the evening sky.
From my high tower, who now will carry my message so
    far away?
My sorrow is drawn out, endless as silk floss.

Too much passion results in too many entanglements.
I can no longer get free from it.
Once more it is the Day of Cold Food.
The swings along the neighboring lanes are stilled.
People sit quietly watching the brilliant moon
Rise and drench the pear blossoms with its rays.

ATTRIBUTED TO LI CH'ING-CHAO

33

THOUGHTS FROM THE WOMEN'S QUARTER

TO THE TUNE "THE BOAT OF STARS"

Year after year I have watched
My jade mirror. Now my rouge
And cream sicken me. It is one more
Year that he has not come back.
My flesh shakes when a letter
Comes from South of the river.
I cannot drink wine since he left,
But sorrow has drunk up all my tears.
I have lost my mind, far-off
In the jungle mists of the South.
The gates of Heaven are nearer
Than the body of my beloved.

ATTRIBUTED TO LI CH'ING-CHAO

EXILE

Breeze soft, sun frail, spring still early.
In a new lined dress my heart was refreshed,
But when I rose from sleep I felt a chill.
I put plum blossoms in my hair.
Now they are withered.
Where is my homeland?
I forget it only when drunk.
The sandalwood incense burned out while I slept.
Now the perfume has gone,
But the wine has not gone.

THE WU-T'UNG TREE

TO THE TUNE "REMEMBERING THE GIRL OF CH'IN"

I stand on a high tower
And look out over jumbled mountains
And wilderness plains
And thin gleaming mist—
Thin gleaming mist.
As the ravens fly home to roost,
Bugles ring out against the sunset sky.
The incense has faded,
But some wine remains.
My arms embrace nothing but remorse.
The wu-t'ung leaves fall—
The wu-t'ung leaves fall.
Autumn colors return.
My desolation returns.

CASSIA FLOWERS

TO A NEW VERSION OF "THE SILK WASHING BROOK"

The twisted limbs break
Into ten thousand flecks of gold,
On layer upon layer of carved jade leaves,
Fresh and bright as the grace of Yen Fu.
The heaps of plum petals seem vulgar.
The lilacs seem coarse and contorted.
Your perfume has broken into
My sorrowful dream of the one
A thousand miles away,
And left me drained of emotion.

BANANA TREES

TO THE TUNE "PICKING MULBERRIES"

Who planted banana trees in front of my window?
Their shadows fall in the midst of the courtyard.
Their shadows fall in the midst of the courtyard.
Leaves like hearts, leaves like hearts,
That open and close with excess of love.
Midnight, rain on the leaves saddens my own heart.
Dien! Di! Dien! Di! Bitter cold, unceasing rain.
Drip! Drop! Drip! Drop! Bitter cold, unceasing rain.
Loneliness. Loneliness.
Sorrow corrodes this exile from the North.
How can I bear to lie awake and listen?

The chilly sun climbs up the window catches.
The wu-t'ung tree should hate last night's frost.
The wine is all drunk so I make the best of bitter tea.
My dream interrupted, the fragrance of Dragon incense
Must take its place.
Autumn is ended but the day is still too long.
I am more lonely and homesick
Than Chung Hsüan.
It is better to accept my fate.
Drunk in front of my wine cup;
I should not be ungrateful
For the yellow chrysanthemums
Along the Eastern Wall.

PLUM BLOSSOMS

The courtyard is deep, profoundly deep.
The windows are cloudy.
The rooms are foggy.
Spring is late.
For whom has my fragrant beauty withered?
Last night you appeared in my dreams.
The trees of the South must be all in bloom.
Frail as jade, ethereal as sandalwood perfume,
Our love will last always.
O Tatar flute on the South Tower
Do not blow.
You will blow away the rich perfume.
The wind grows warm.
The sun shines longer.
We will be separated
Till the apricots bloom.

I GAVE A PARTY TO MY RELATIVES
ON THE DAY OF PURIFICATION

TO THE TUNE "BUTTERFLIES LOVE FLOWERS"

Tranquil and serene, the night
Seems to last forever.
Yet we are seldom happy.
We all dream of Ch'ang An
And long to take the road back to the capital,
And see this year again the beauty of Spring, come with
Moonlight and shadow on the new flowers.
Although the food is simple, as are the cups,
The wine is good, the plums sour.
That is enough to satisfy us.
We drink and deck our hair with flowers
But do not laugh,
For we and the Spring grow old.

FADING PLUM BLOSSOMS

Spring is hidden in my studio,
Daylight locked out of my window.
My painted room is profoundly secluded.
The seal character incense is burned out.
The shadows of the sunset
Descend across the curtain hooks.
Now that the wild plum I planted myself
Is blooming so well this year
I do not need to climb the waterfall
Seeking wild plum blossoms.
No one comes to visit me.
I am as lonely as ever was Ho Sun in Yang Chou.
I know that although my plum blossoms
Are lovelier than all others
The rain will soon scatter them in disorder,
And the wind pluck them away.
The sound of a horizontal flute fills the whole house
With a melody of dense sorrow.
I will not feel badly when their perfume dissolves
And their jade snow petals fall.
When they have all been swept away
The memory of my love for them will remain.
It is difficult to describe the beauty of their shadows
Cast by the pale moonlight.

SPRING FADES

Spring fades. Why should I suffer so much from home-
    sickness?
I am ill. Combing my long hair exasperates me.
Under the roof beams the swallows chatter too much all
    day long.
A soft breeze fills the curtains with the perfume of roses.

HIS DEATH

There are fragrant plants around the pond
In the deep green shade of the garden.
As the sun declines
A chill seeps through the gauze window.
The jade curtain hooks and the gold locks of the doors
Keep out any possible guests.
I sit at my table facing a wine cup,
Alone with my sorrow for him
At the corner of the ocean
And the edge of heaven.
I cannot keep the blackberry petals from falling.
I have only the pear blossoms to comfort me.
In the years that were gone we were happy together.
Light filled our lives like incense in our sleeves.
We drank tea together, made over the living fire.
We went out together on the festivals
Among the writhing dragons, on our beloved horses
In the stream of carriages, unafraid of sudden storms.
We toasted each other in warm wine,
And wrote poems on flowered paper.
Now I wonder if we will
Ever embrace one another again.
Will the good days ever return?

I SMELL THE FRAGRANCE OF WITHERED
PLUM BLOSSOMS BY MY PILLOW

TO THE TUNE "UNBURDENING ONESELF"

Last night, so very drunk,
I fell asleep in make-up and jewelry,
Withered plum blossoms still in my hair.
The fumes of wine and blossoms saturated my dream of
     Spring,
And finally broke through and woke me up.
I could not return to dreams of far-off love.
Everyone was still.
Under the declining moon,
I unrolled the kingfisher-green curtain,
Crumpled the fallen petals,
Lit the remaining incense,
And confronted the passing hours.

SPRING ENDS

TO THE TUNE "SPRING AT WU LING"

The gentle breeze has died down.
The perfumed dust has settled.
It is the end of the time
Of flowers. Evening falls
And all day I have been too
Lazy to comb my hair.

Our furniture is just the same.
He no longer exists.
All effort would be wasted.
Before I can speak,
My tears choke me.
I hear that Spring at Two Rivers
Is still beautiful.
I had hoped to take a boat there,
But I know so fragile a vessel
Won't bear such a weight of sorrow.

TO THE TUNE "A SONG OF THE SOUTH"

The River of Heaven turns across the sky.
All the world is covered with bed curtains.
It grows cold.
Tear stains spread on my mat and pillow.
I get up and take off my clothes
And listlessly ask "How late at night is it?"
The green feather pattern of lotus pods,
The gold thread design of lotus leaves,
Seem small and sparse on my gauze sleeping robe.
The same weather as in the old days,
The same dress I wore then,
Only my arms are empty of love,
And our past is gone forever.

A SONG OF DEPARTURE

Warm rain and soft breeze by turns
Have just broken
And driven away the chill.
Moist as the pussy willows,
Light as the plum blossoms,
Already I feel the heart of Spring vibrating.
But now who will share with me
The joys of wine and poetry?
Tears streak my rouge.
My hairpins are too heavy.
I put on my new quilted robe
Sewn with gold thread
And throw myself against a pile of pillows,
Crushing my phoenix hairpins.
Alone, all I can embrace is my endless sorrow.
I know a good dream will never come.
So I stay up till past midnight
Trimming the lamp flower's smoking wick.

ON PLUM BLOSSOMS

TO THE TUNE "A LITTLE WILD GOOSE"

This morning I woke
In a bamboo bed with paper curtains.
I have no words for my weary sorrow,
No fine poetic thoughts.
The sandalwood incense smoke is stale,
The jade burner is cold.
I feel as though I were filled with quivering water.
To accompany my feelings
Someone plays three times on a flute
"Plum Blossoms Are Falling
in a Village by the River."
How bitter this Spring is.
Small wind, fine rain, *hsiao, hsiao,*
Falls like a thousand lines of tears.
The flute player is gone.
The jade tower is empty.
Broken hearted—we had relied on each other.
I pick a plum branch,
But my man has gone beyond the sky,
And there is no one to give it to.

WRITTEN BY CHANCE

Fifteen years ago, beneath moonlight and flowers,
I walked with you
We composed flower-viewing poems together.
Tonight the moonlight and flowers are just the same
But how can I ever hold in my arms the same love.

POLITICS

SENTIMENT

On the tenth of the eighth month, in the third reign year of Hsüan-hê (1121), I arrived at the yamen in Lai County. I sat in my small room and looked around. Nothing from the collection I had cherished all my lifetime was there. I opened a rhyme book on the table aimlessly, and told myself I would compose a poem with the rhyme on whatever page I turned. It was *tze,* so I wrote a poem on "Sentiment" with the rhyme *tze.*

The cold air soaks through the window.
Around this broken desk
I can find no books of literature or history.
The ancient warrior Yüan Shu
Was trapped here long ago.
He said, "Is this place where I meet my end?"
The public officials in Ch'ing State
All love money like a brother.
They enjoy making trouble for themselves
And hurry-scurry all day long.
I lock my doors and turn away
The visitors so that I can compose a poem.
In the little bedroom the fragrance
Of incense seems to congeal as my thoughts take shape.
I find my most trustworthy friends in solitude:
Mr. Nonexistence and Scholar No Such.

POEMS ON YÜEN CHIEH'S "ODE TO THE RESTORATION OF T'ANG" TO RHYME WITH CHANG WEN-CH'IEN'S POEM

I

Fifty years of achievement passed like a lightning flash.
Now the flowers and willows in your Bright Flower
    Palace
Are overgrown and gone to weeds,
Like the ruins of the long gone capital, Hsien Yang.
The grooms of your five stables
And kennels for hunting dogs and hawks,
And the trainers of your fighting cocks,
Grew befuddled with wine and too much food,
And never realized they were growing old.
Troops of the Northern Barbarians
Suddenly appeared, as if dropped from Heaven.
The rebel Turk An Lu-shan turned out
To be an able scoundrel and a general of talent.
Tatar horses paraded in front of your Banquet Hall,
And trampled pearls and emeralds into fragrant dust.
Your counterattacking troops were scattered
Like weeds in a whirlwind.
They say your best cavalry horses had died in the relays
That brought fresh lichees from the South.
Once Your Majesty's merits and virtues
Were like those of the ancient sage kings Yao and Shun,
And even the Emperor of Heaven.
What good did it do to write your praises in trivial odes?
What a waste of time it was for great artists
To polish the rocks on the cliffs and engrave your virtues.

Your generals Kuo Tzu-yi and Li Kuang-pi fought
     loyally.
The Mandate of Heaven passed from you,
But then regretted the calamity it had sent down.
The minds of men gradually became unclouded.
The fall of Hsia Dynasty and Shang mirrored your own
     fate.
And you should have been far
More cautious, self-educated by the past.
The ancient bamboo books of history
Were there for you to study.
You didn't see that
Your prime minister Chang Shuo
Was a master of many strategies,
He lost everything but his life, betrayed by his rival Yao
     Ts'ung.

II

Who has not heard the amazing story
Of the astonishing downfall and restoration
During the reign of Ming Huang?
Now grass and weeds have overgrown
This monument to the restoration.
No one knew the country had been betrayed
To a formidable enemy,
But went on praising the successes of the ministers.

Who sent the Imperial Concubine down from Heaven?
Her sisters, Duchesses of Kuo, Ch'in, and Han,

Were also richly gifted by Heaven.
When flower, mulberry, Turkish drums, and jade chimes
began to play,
The Spring breeze dared not raise a speck of dust.

Today who still remembers
Even the names of An Lu-shan and Shih Ssu-ming?
Young warriors and fierce generals peacefully sleep in
death.
This peak, shaped like an urn, is so high that it nearly
reaches Heaven.
On the top are chiseled the titles and praises of the
Emperor.
Times change, power passes;
It is the pity of the world.
The hearts of the vicious were
Deep chasms of evil.
At last he was able to return home.
Ten thousand miles from Szechwan.
But once he was driven out of the Southern Palace,
The doors closed behind him, never to open.
How unjust, that although the filial virtue
Of the Emperor was great as Heaven,
His generals claimed all the credit.
Alas Eunuch Kao Li-shih did not caution him of
Li Fu-kuo's manipulation and conspiracy with the new
Empress,
All he could remember is the Spring in Chang An
When shepherd's-purse sold by the peck.

POEMS DEDICATED TO LORD HAN, THE MINISTER
OF THE COUNCIL OF DEFENSE, AND LORD HU,
THE MINISTER OF THE BOARD OF WORKS
[With a subtitle]

In the fifth month of the third reign year of Shao-hsing
(1133), Lord Han, the Minister of the Council of Defense,
and Lord Hu, the Minister of the Board of Works, were
appointed as envoys to the Barbarians, in order to establish
communication between our Supreme Lord and our captive
Emperor Hui and Emperor Ch'in. I am a married woman,
style-name Ease and Peace Scholar. Both my father and
grandfather were pupils of Lord Han's ancestors. Today the
fame of my clan has declined, and our family members are
scattered among the humble and the insignificant. I dare not
lift up my head to look at the dust raised by the carriages of
Your Lordship. In addition, I am striken by poverty and ail-
ments. Fortunately, my spirit has not yet deteriorated. When
I heard of this Imperial decree, I was unable to withhold my
voice any longer. Therefore, I have composed two poems in
the ancient regular form, to express my trivial thoughts and
to prepare poems for a future collector of my poetry.

I. TO LORD HAN

It is the summer in the sixth month of the seventh year
    of your reign.
Your Majesty has held audience in the court for many
    years.
You watch the dense clouds in the South through the
    tassels of pearls hanging down from your crown.

59

Your royal robe droops on the floor as you contemplate a
    Northern expedition.
I, gratified, seem to hear that Your Majesty spoke in the
    court:
"Generals of the Frontier, Governors of the Provinces,
    and Court Officials,
Hundreds of years have gone by, there must be a very
    virtuous man among you.
Now that we have survived an extremely perilous time,
I do not look for a man to drive the Tatars far North
    like General Tou who erected a monument at Yen
    Jan Mountain;
Nor do I look for a man to establish a military colony in
    the far West as General Chao who planted willows
    in the Golden City.
Is there a single official here with profound filial thoughts?
Who can understand me, longing for my parents as the
    grass bends for dew?
I will no longer avoid drinking meat soup because it
    reminds me that my mother must be hungry in exile,
For now I can give orders to use the grease for the axles
    of the carriage for my envoys.
In exchange for my parents I am willing to give up land,
And jade and silk are but dust to me.
Who among you will receive this Imperial mission?
He should take an abundance of money along and his
    deliverance of my message should be extremely
    humble."
Four generals answered in unison:
"Your Majesty knows thoroughly all your subject officials.

Among the ministers of the interior court, he is peerless.
Like Han Yü of the T'ang Dynasty who heads the Board
of Education,
He is outstanding even among the One Hundred
Scholars.
His conduct is the model for a million people.
During the reign of Emperor Jen and Emperor Hui,
He was as virtuous as the ancient sage ministers Kao and
K'uei.
Like Wang Shang who overawed the Huns,
Like General Tzu-yi who was revered by the Turks,
He has already dispersed the courage of the Barbarians.
This lord is the most suitable man to receive the mission."
The lord prostrated himself and saluted His Majesty,
And received the mission on the white marble platform.
He said, "No matter how difficult it is, your subject dare
not decline such a decree
Because this is a moment of utmost urgency.
I will not consult the opinions of my family,
Nor will I bid farewell to my wife and sons.
I uphold in reverence the spirit of Heaven and Earth, and
I uphold in reverence the augustness of our Imperial
Ancestor's shrine,
Carrying your Imperial decree sealed by purple paste,
I will enter straightforwardly Yellow Dragon City, the
Tatar capital.
The Barbarian chief will certainly prostrate and kowtow
to it,
Their nobles will all come out to greet it.

Only the most kind Supreme Lord, like Your Majesty,
would offer such trust to them.

Therefore, the hot-blooded youth should refrain for a
while from joining in the army, to wear the red
tassels, for

If the situation permits, I would dip the brush in the
blood of dog and horse,

And sign a treaty with them, that will last like Heaven
and Earth."

II. TO LORD HU

The integrity of Lord Hu is rare and incomparable.

With great calm and confidence you will negotiate peace.

Your heart is warm, for you have put on the garment
which His Majesty took off from himself and
bestowed on you.

Do not sing a sad farewell song like Ching K'o's verse
lamenting the cold water of River Yi.

Many days now the sky has been cloudy and the earth
damp.

The driving rain has not yet calmed down, and the wind
is still blowing hard.

As your cart rattles by and your horse neighs *hsiao, hsiao,*

Brave men and cowards will be moved to tears.

Even I, an ignorant widow, who live among commoners,

Dare to send in this poem, with my heart bleeding, to
His Majesty's secretary.

The Barbarians are by nature cruel as tigers and wolves.

Best be on guard for unforeseen dangers.

Long ago during the negotiation between Sung and Ch'u states, the insincere Ch'u generals hid weapons inside their gowns.
Before you climb up the city wall to attend the meeting, please remember that the Turks once tried to change
The place of the conferences so that they could ambush the T'ang army.
K'uei Ch'iu and Chien T'u, where crucial peace conferences in the past were held, have not yet become ruins.
Do not look down upon diplomats and scholars.
At the request of his lord, Yüan Hung, without even dismounting from his horse, had immediately completed a long eulogy of the victory.
When Prince Meng-ch'ang ran in flight to the Yao Han Pass at midnight, his followers mimicked the cock's cry so well that the guards opened the gates and let them pass through.
A skillful carpenter never throws away any timber, including twisted chestnut oak.
One could be benefitted even from the words of a woodcutter.

We shall not ask for the precious pearl of the Duke of Sui, nor for the priceless jade disk of Master Ho.
We merely ask for the recent news of our homeland.
The Palace of Spiritual Illumination must be still there, surrounded by desolation.
What's happened to the stone statues buried deep in grass, still guarding the Imperial tombs?

Is it true that our people left behind in the occupied
territories are still planting mulberry trees and hemp?
Is it true that the rear guard of the Barbarians only
patrols the city walls?

This widow's father and grandfather were born in
Shantung.
Although they never held high office, their fame spread
wide and far.
I remember when they carried on animated discussions
with other scholars by the city gate,
The listeners were so crowded that their sweat fell like
rain.
Their offspring crossed the Yangtse River to the South
many years ago.
Drifting in the rapids, they mingled with refugees.
I send blood-stained tears to the mountains and rivers of
home,
And sprinkle a cup of earth on East Mountain.
I imagine when Your Lordship, His Majesty's envoy,
upholding the Imperial spirit, passes through our
two capitals, K'ai Feng and Lo Yang,
Thousands of people would line the streets and present
tea and broth to welcome you.
The peach trees in the Palace of Everlasting Prosperity
will bloom all over.
The magpies on the Flower Calyx Tower will no longer
flutter in dismay.
Announce that the Emperor's heart aches for the suffering
people—they are his own children.

Let them understand that the Will of Heaven remembers
    all living beings.
Our sagacious Emperor offers his trust which is as bril-
    liant as the sun.
There is no need to negotiate many times after the long
    chaos of the years.

A SATIRE ON THE LORDS
WHO CROSSED THE YANGTSE
IN FLIGHT FROM THE CHIN TROOPS

Alive we need heroes among the living
Who when dead will be heroes among the ghosts.
I cannot tell how much we miss Hsiang Yü
Who preferred death to crossing to the East of the River.

ON HISTORY

The Later Han Dynasty succeeded the Former.
In between them the House of Hsin was only an excres-
cence.
That is why the poet Chi K'ang denounced
The Shang and Chou dynasties until his death.

WRITTEN ON CLIMBING EIGHT POEMS TOWER

Five hundred years ago Shen Yüeh
Wrote eight elegant poems
Celebrating this tower by the river.
Now this gracious man is gone forever.
He left the rivers and mountains
For our meditation.
The waters under the tower reach
Three thousand miles into the Southern Kingdom.
The tower guards the river towns of fourteen counties.

OUR BOAT STARTS AT NIGHT
FROM THE BEACH OF YEN KUANG

Great ships sail only for profit.
Only small boats come here because of your fame.
The passers-by are embarrassed by your virtue.
So in the night we steal by the place where you used to
    fish.

IN THE EMPEROR'S CHAMBER

As the sun and moon,
Your greatness matches the Golden Age of Yao.
You are steadfast as the North Pole,
Wise as the ancient king, Shun.
In your army camps there are many officers
Brilliant and wise.

It is not enough to present our lord
Bamboo mats threaded with gold,
Or jade couches with twisted carved legs.
The scent of burning torches
Comes on the Spring wind.
This is no time to light aloes wood incense.

TO THE EMPRESS

Midsummer is the best time
To present to you poems on the festival,
For Your Highness has just finished
Supervising the rearing of silkworms.
Now the grooms are busy breeding
Horses in the golden Imperial stables.
I wish ten thousand years
Of life for our Supreme Lord,
And may Your Highness see many sons.

TO AN IMPERIAL LADY

In three palaces everybody is busy
Getting ready for the new feast
Of the Fifth Day of the Fifth Month.
Before dawn the women have already finished
Making up their faces and doing elaborate coiffures
Decorated with flowers.
His Highness writes a poem on a girl's fan.
She covers her face with it flirtatiously.
Then he gives that verse to be sung for the holiday.

TO THE IMPERIAL CONCUBINE

You will give birth to a Prince.
Now the gold bracelet of honor shines on your arm.
Like Lady Kou Yi of the Han Dynasty
Your son will succeed to the throne.
You will be equal to the Empress
In the Bright Sun Palace.
Spring will be born in
Your jeweled bed curtains of juniper seeds
Where the Emperor drinks delight
From his everlasting jade cup.

MYSTICISM

DREAM

TO THE TUNE "THE HONOR OF A FISHERMAN"

The heavens join with the clouds.
The billowing clouds merge in fog.
As the dawn approaches in the River of Heaven,
A thousand sails are dancing.
I am rapt away to the place of the Supreme,
And hear the words of Heaven
Asking me where I am going.
I answer, "It is a long road, alas,
Finally I've come to where the sun sets."
I try to put into verse my experience
But my words only amaze me.
The huge roc bird is flying
On a ninety-thousand-mile wind.
O wind, do not stop
Until my little boat has been blown
To the Immortal Islands
In the Eastern Sea.

WRITTEN ON THE SEVENTH DAY
OF THE SEVENTH MONTH
TO THE TUNE "YOU MOVE IN FRAGRANCE"

Deep in the grass the crickets sing.
Wu-t'ung leaves fall suddenly and startle me.
Sorrow lies thick
On the ways of men and high Heaven.
On the cloud stairs to the floor of moonlight
The doors are all locked for a thousand miles.
Even if our floating rafts could come and go
We could not meet each other,
Nor cross the star bridge of magpies.
Once a year the Cowboy and Weaving Girl meet.
Imagine the year-long bitterness of their parting.
Now suddenly in the midst of their love-making
The wind blows first clear and then rain.

A MORNING DREAM

This morning I dreamed I followed
Widely spaced bells, ringing in the wind,
And climbed through mists to rosy clouds.
I realized my destined affinity
With An Ch'i-sheng the ancient sage.
I met unexpectedly O Lü-hua
The heavenly maiden.
The Autumn wind was just then untrustworthy
And blew away all the Jade Well Flowers.
Together we saw lotus roots as big as boats.
Together we ate jujubes as huge as melons.
We were the guests of those on swaying lotus seats.
They spoke in splendid language,
Full of subtle meanings.
They argued with sharp words over paradoxes.
We drank tea brewed on living fire.
Although this might not help the Emperor to govern,
It is endless happiness.
The life of men could be like this.
Why did I have to return to my former home,
Wake up, dress, sit in meditation.
Cover my ears to shut out the disgusting racket.
My heart knows I can never see my dream come true.
At least I can remember
That world and sigh.

OLD AGE

Year after year in the snow, intoxicated,
I have put the new plum blossoms
In my hair.
Now the fallen petals
Only depress me.
All I have gained is a dress
Wet with crystal tears.
This year I am at the corner
Of the sea and the edge of Heaven.
I am old and lonely.
My temples have turned white.
I realize that the evening wind
Is too strong for me.
It is no longer possible
For me to contemplate
The blossoming plums.

CASSIA FLOWERS

TO A NEW VERSION OF "THE SILK WASHING BROOK"

After my sickness
My temples have turned gray.
I lie and watch the waning moon
Climb up the gauze window screen.
I boil a drink of cardamom leaf tips
Instead of tea.
It is good to rest on my pillows
And write poetry.
Before the door
Beautiful in wind, shadow and rain,
All day the fragrant cassia blossoms
Bend toward me, delicate and subtle.

AT A POETRY PARTY I AM GIVEN THE RHYME *CHIH*

Although I've studied poetry for thirty years
I try to keep my mouth shut and avoid reputation.
Now who is this nosy gentleman talking about my poetry
Like Yang Ching-chih
Who spoke of Hsiang Ssu everywhere he went.

TO THE TUNE "IMMORTALS ON THE RIVER BANK"

How deep, profoundly deep, the courtyard is.
The windows are cloudy.
Fog penetrates the closed rooms.
Pussy willows and plum buds begin to show,
As Spring returns to the trees of Nanking.
I grow old in this old city.
Songs of love, moon, and wind are gone
With the past.
I am old and have accomplished little.
No one cares for me now.
I wither away like last year's
Scattered leaves.
I have no desire to light the lantern,
No desire to walk in the last snow.

The sun sets in molten gold.
The evening clouds form a jade disk.
Where is he?
Dense white mist envelops the willows.
A sad flute plays "Falling Plum Blossoms."
How many Spring days are left now?
This Feast of Lanterns should be joyful.
The weather is calm and lovely.
But who can tell if it
Will be followed by wind and rain?
A friend sends her perfumed carriage
And high-bred horses to fetch me.
I decline the invitation of
My old poetry and wine companion.
I remember the happy days in the lost capital.
We took our ease in the women's quarters.
The Feast of Lanterns was elaborately celebrated—
Gold pendants, emerald hairpins, brocaded girdles,
New sashes—we competed
To see who was most smartly dressed.
Now I am withering away,
Wind-blown hair, frosty temples.
I am embarrassed to go out this evening
Among girls in the flower of youth.
I prefer to stay beyond the curtains,
And listen to talk and laughter
I can no longer share.

Li Ch'ing-chao (1084–c.1151) is universally considered to be China's greatest woman poet. Her life was colorful and versatile: other than a great poet, she was a scholar of history and classics, a literary critic, an art collector, a specialist in bronze and stone inscriptions, a painter, a calligrapher, and a political commentator. Li is reputed to be the greatest writer of *tz'u* poetry, a lyric verse form written to the popular tunes of the Sung Dynasty (960–1279). Her *tz'u* poems are full of lucid imagery, refined and highly suggestive. In this collection we have translated all her *tz'u* poems. Her poems in *shih* form, the formal, regular verse, were widely read by her contemporaries. But today, only seventeen of her *shih* poems can be found.[1]

Li Ch'ing-chao and her husband Chao Ming-ch'eng came from well-known families of scholars and officials. Wang Kung-ch'en (1012–85), the grandfather of Ch'ing-chao's mother, was a prime minister.[2] Her mother had some reputation as a poet. Her father, Li Ke-fei, was an avid prose writer and a member of the prominent and powerful literary circle led by Su Tung-p'o. When she was a child, her father was a professor and administrator in the Imperial Academy in the capital, K'ai Feng. They lived in a house surrounded by dense bamboo groves where her father often entertained his literary friends.[3]

As a young girl, Ch'ing-chao already displayed her talents and untamed spirit. When she was about seventeen, she wrote two poems in *shih* form to rhyme with a poem written by Chang Lei (Chang Wen-ch'ien), a good friend of Li Ke-fei, on the newly discovered monument erected in the eighth century for the restoration of the court after the An Lu-shan rebellion.[4] For a girl to compete with her father's friend by writing poems was certainly not considered modest. In her poem, she even dared to criticize the shallowness of Chang's view that he merely saw the success of General Kuo Tzu-yi, totally ignoring the complexity of the cause and effect of a historical event. According to the Confucian code for women in the elite society, her conduct and ideas were unruly. However, since most of her father's literary friends were open-minded and unconventional, they not only appreciated her talents, but encouraged her creativity.[5] Brought up in such a favorable environment, her great potential began to take form.

When she was eighteen she married Chao Ming-ch'eng, a student in the Imperial Academy. He was the youngest son of Chao T'ing-chih, who was an ambitious politician of great influence. For a thousand years, their marriage has been celebrated by the literary gentry as an ideal one. They wrote poems to each other. They shared the same passion for poetry and classics, music, painting, and the art of calligraphy. Ch'ing-chao herself describes their humble but delightful life:

My husband was twenty-one then, studying at the Imperial Academy. Both the Chao and Li families were not wealthy. Our lives had been modest and thrifty. On the first and the fifteenth of each month, when he was granted leave of absence from school, he used to pawn his clothes for five hundred copper coins so that he could buy fruit and rubbings of stone inscriptions from the market at the Hsiang

Kuo Temple. After he brought them home, the two of us would taste the fruit and study the rubbings. We enjoyed ourselves so much that we claimed ourselves the citizens of the ancient ideal state of Ko T'ien.[6]

Ch'ing-chao must have somewhat exaggerated the strenuous conditions of their financial state, for in one of her poems, she appeared to be a young woman dressing up in the most fashionable and luxurious way:

I remember the happy days in the lost capital.
We took our ease in the women's quarters.
The Feast of Lanterns was elaborately celebrated—
Gold pendants, emerald hairpins, brocaded girdles,
New sashes—we competed
To see who was most smartly dressed.[7]

Ch'ing-chao the young bride was apparently lively, radiant, and enjoyed her married life. Her poems written in this period are vivid and sensuous. They portray a lovely, witty, and coquettish young lady.

However, the life of the newlyweds was not as idyllic as it has been extolled in the past. In fact, their life was full of tension and stress because of their close linkage to the ruthless power struggle in the court. About thirty years before Ch'ing-chao and Ming-ch'eng were married, the officials in the Sung court were divided into two rival factions. In 1070 when the emperor appointed Wang An-shih prime minister, Wang's new faction seized power in the court. The old factions soon formed an alliance to oppose Wang's programs of reformation. These old factions were led by outstanding statesmen and writers, such as Ssu-ma Kuang and Su Tung-p'o. Whenever one group seized power, they always strove to wipe out members of the other group from the court, by sending them into exile or imprisoning them. This power struggle between the new and the old factions lasted until the fall of the Northern Sung Dynasty in 1126.

Li Ke-fei, Ch'ing-chao's father, had been a follower of Su Tung-p'o, and a steady member of the old faction. On the other hand, Chao T'ing-chih, though befriended by some members of the old faction, had been a political enemy of Su Tung-p'o ever since Ch'ing-chao and Ming-ch'eng were little children.[8] Chao T'ing-chih gradually drifted away from the old faction and finally, in the year 1101, sided with Ts'ai Ching (1047–1126), the notorious leader of the new faction. This was exactly the year Ch'ing-chao became a bride of the Chao family. Thus, she must have felt traces of hostility in the new environment, for her father and her father-in-law were respectively aligned with two rival parties.

After she was wedded, Ch'ing-chao and Ming-ch'eng lived in the capital for seven turbulent years. In 1102, the second year of her marriage, Li's father-in-law became the vice prime minister. Meanwhile, Prime Minister Ts'ai Ching expelled seventeen members of the old faction from the capital. Li Ke-fei was among them. Ch'ing-chao was so upset about her father's political disgrace that she presented poems to her father-in-law, beseeching him to save her father. During this period, poetry was an influential medium; when a poem was widely circulated among the gentry, it could exercise a certain pressure on public opinion. Only fragments of the poems she wrote to her father-in-law can be found today. She describes the political struggle as "Your fingers are burned while your heart turns cold." In the third year of her marriage, an imperial decree was proclaimed throughout the kingdom stating that all books written by Su Tung-p'o should be burned, that the sons of the expelled officials were not allowed to attend the audience in the palace, and that marriage between the royal family and the family members of the expelled officials was forbidden. Ch'ing-chao, as a family member of an expelled official, must have felt deeply humiliated.

The fifth year of their marriage was a relative relief: because of an amnesty, Li Ke-fei was called back to the court. Meanwhile, the emperor appointed Chao T'ing-chih prime minister of the Right, and dismissed Ts'ai Ching from the office of the prime minister of the Left. By this time, Chao T'ing-chih and Ts'ai Ching's relationship had already turned sour. Thus, Chao T'ing-chih won another political victory and became the most powerful official in the kingdom. Unfortunately, next year in 1107, the Chao family underwent a catastrophe. In the first month of the year, Ts'ai Ching was reappointed the prime minister of the Left. Two months later, Chao T'ing-chih fell in disfavor with the emperor and was dismissed from the office of the prime minister. Sixteen days thereafter, he died of an illness. Deprived of its protector, the Chao family was doomed. Chao T'ing-chih's political enemy, Ts'ai Ching, decided to persecute his family members now that he was dead. Ts'ai accused Chao T'ing-chih of receiving large sums of bribery. The emperor thus deprived Chao T'ing-chih of his honorary titles and imprisoned Chao's family members in the capital and his relatives in Ch'ing Chou, their home town in

Shantung Province. Ming-ch'eng must have been arrested and interrogated. A few months later, the Chao family was released because their political enemies could not find any substantial criminal evidence to charge them with. However, the political life of Ming-ch'eng and his brothers came to an end, for from then on Ts'ai Ching was favored continually by the emperor. Between the ages of nineteen and twenty-five, therefore, Ch'ing-chao experienced to the full extent the ups and downs of the power struggle in the court. However, these experiences did not cool down her interest in politics. In fact, years later she wrote politically satiric poems with an even greater zest than before.

Although Ming-ch'eng became a political outcast for more than ten years, they lived happily in Ch'ing Chou. At last they could fully indulge themselves in their hobbies: collecting and cataloging paintings, calligraphy, the casted inscriptions on the ceremonial bronze vessels of Shang (eighteenth to twelfth centuries B.C.) and Chou (twelfth to third centuries B.C.), rubbings of essays carved on stone monuments, rare books, manuscripts, etc. Ch'ing-chao herself thus describes incidents of their happy life:

> Whenever paintings or calligraphic works were bought, they rolled and unrolled the scrolls time and again. Whenever an ancient wine pot was acquired, they examined it with great attention. They corrected the mistakes in the books, pointed out the faults in the antiques, and limited the time of appreciation to the burning of one candle. Every evening, after dinner, they sat together and played a game they had invented themselves in front of a

pile of books. The game consisted of pointing out in which volume, on which page, and in which line such or such an event was mentioned. The one who guessed correctly was the winner and had the privilege of taking a sip of the jasmine tea. Sometimes they enjoyed themselves so immensely and laughed so much that they caused the tea cup to tumble from their laps.[9]

Eventually, because of their tireless search and of their discriminating selection, their collection became one of the finest and largest in the nation. It filled ten huge storage rooms in Ch'ing Chou. They also collaborated in editing the most comprehensive work ever written on ancient inscriptions: *The Study of Bronze and Stone Inscriptions.* Her hobbies and activities, such as scholarly research and the collecting of art, were unusual indeed, for they were exclusively reserved for the gentry and officials, not for their wives. She was, without question, the most "liberated" woman of her time.

After thirteen years of retirement, in the year 1121, Ming-ch'eng returned to the bureaucratic world. It seems Ts'ai Ching's hostility toward the Chao family had diminished by that time. During the following four years, Ming-ch'eng was appointed successively the local magistrate of two counties in Shantung Province. However, Ming-ch'eng spent most of his time enlarging and studying his collection, instead of working in his office. During the period they lived in Ch'ing Chou, Ming-ch'eng used to take trips to the mountains just to search for old monuments. He carried on this search even when he was a magistrate. Ch'ing-chao's *tz'u* poems about her loneliness and the sorrow of departure were probably written during his trips. In ancient times, women of the elite society were not allowed to travel as freely as men. Therefore, when Ming-ch'eng took trips, she had to stay home. These poems were permeated with intense feelings which, however, were dispersed into the objects around the persona. Instead of explicitly crying out her grief, she expressed it through projecting her feelings into her environment in the form of crystal imagery. In her loneliness, her love for wine seemed to be the only consolation. Intoxication liberated her sensory perception to the full. She became extremely sensitive to the subtle changes in her environment and to the transiency of time. In her famous poem, "A Weary Song to a Slow Sad Tune," when she consumed two or three cups of wine, her five senses were sharpened. The evening breeze becomes piercing, the wild goose brings back her sad memory, the fallen flowers grieve her, the darkness outside the window oppresses her, and the splashes of raindrops on the leaves almost tear her nerves. The beautiful, fascinating sensory imagery in her *tz'u* poetry owes much to this special predilection of hers.

In 1127 the Tatars from Manchuria plundered the capital K'ai Feng and brought back to the North as trophies the Sung emperors and most of the royal family. The empire was shattered into pieces. Ch'ing-chao suffered tremendously in this chaotic state of affairs. Before the fall of the capital, Ming-ch'eng had already gone to Nanking, a city south of the Yangtse River, to attend his mother's funeral. Meanwhile, he moved south the most valuable portion of their collection. Ch'ing-chao was left behind in Ch'ing Chou to take care of their household and the remainder of their collection. Soon after the capital was taken by the Tatars, the Sung army stationed at Ch'ing Chou staged a mutiny in which the governor was killed. Ch'ing-chao was forced to flee and make the long journey to Nanking by herself. She had left behind the treasures so dear to their hearts. At the end of this year, the Tatar troops took Ch'ing Chou. They burned the civilian houses in the city. Ch'ing-chao and Ming-ch'eng's collection, in the ten storage rooms, all went up in flames.

The following spring, after months of flight, Ch'ing-chao finally reached Nanking to join her husband, who in the meantime had been appointed the city magistrate of Nanking. She must have encountered many terrifying experiences during her journey, but these did not break her spirit. Being a fervent patriot, she scorned the members in the court who persuaded the new emperor, Kao Tsung, to flee to the South, instead of assisting him to resist the Tatars. Her poems of political satire were widely read by her contemporaries. These lines are fragments from one of her lost poems:

> Among the gentry who have fled to the South
> We do not have Wang Tao.
> No news coming from the North
> Brings Liu K'un's victory.

Wang Tao helped Emperor Yüan Ti of the Chin Dynasty to set up a government in the South after the nomads took their capital in the fourth century. Liu K'un, a contemporary of Wang Tao, fought fiercely against the nomads. Ch'ing-chao used these two allusions to attack the lack of talent and ability of the high officials and generals in the Sung court. Her poem, "A Satire on the Lords Who Crossed the Yangtse in Flight from the Chin Troops" implies that there was not even a single courageous man in the army. Her poignant criticism must have won her applause among the patriots, but at the same time antagonized many powerful officials.

During the days when she was the first lady of Nanking, her vigor and love for poetry and for the beauty of nature remained the same. Her relatives in Nanking reported interesting episodes of her life. She would venture to climb up the city walls even in snowstorms, in order to view the distant snow-capped landscape and to capture some poetic inspiration. When, after each excursion, she had completed a poem, she would urge Ming-ch'eng to compose one to rhyme with hers. Ming-ch'eng was compelled to comply with her every time.[10] As the city magistrate of Nanking, Ming-ch'eng could provide his family with a comfortable life and proper protection. However, these sheltered days were brief. The following year, in 1129, Ming-ch'eng fell terribly ill, probably of typhoid, on his way to a new official post. Soon after Ch'ing-chao reached the inn where he was staying, he died. He was forty-nine. After Ch'ing-chao buried him, she was left alone, with their sizable collection of art, in a time of disorder and troubles. The Tatars had just crossed the Yangtse River, and the Sung court fled further south. In the next few years, Ch'ing-chao was continually in flight, following the route of the fleeing court. Without a protector now, she lost almost the entire collection: some items were stolen, some abandoned, and some donated to the Imperial Collection.

In 1132, when she was forty-nine, she settled down

in Lin An (today's Hang Chou), where the Sung court established its new capital. It was during this year that the most controversial incident in her life probably occurred.[11] Gathered from several sources in the books written by her contemporaries, it seems Ch'ing-chao married a minor official, Chang Ju-chou, but divorced him a few months later. During their brief marriage, Chang abused her both verbally and physically. She soon appealed for a divorce, and meanwhile she accused Chang of misappropriating military funds. Her divorce was granted, and Chang was convicted. However, she was also imprisoned: according to the Sung law, a wife who brought a lawsuit against her husband was confined, even though her husband had committed the crime. Scholars in the Ming (1368–1644) and Ch'ing (1644–1911) dynasties attacked these records as sheer fabrications. However, their refutations were mostly groundless. Their opinions were to a large extent conditioned by the much stricter moral code for women imposed by the Neo-Confucianists after the thirteenth century. According to the code, if a woman remarried, she was considered a blemish on the whole clan. The writings of these scholars must have been motivated by their wish that the private life of the greatest *tz'u* poetess be stainless. It was not unlikely, as they had suggested, that Ch'ing-chao's political enemies fabricated this sordid story to ruin her reputation. However, even if she did marry twice, it seems perfectly natural for a lonely, helpless woman to find someone to lean on in such a chaotic period. In the Sung Dynasty, it was rather common for a widow to marry again. The remarried woman was not condemned, as she was later.

As Ch'ing-chao grew older, her *tz'u* poems lost their former vitality and color, but were permeated with a growing sense of reconciliation. Although she had experienced much hardship and many shocks, she was still able to celebrate the beautiful and the artistic, no matter how humble and minute they were. She wrote during her recuperation from an illness in "Cassia Flowers, To a new version of *The Silk Washing Brook*":

> It is good to rest on my pillows.
> And write poetry.
> Before the door
> Beautiful in wind, shadow and rain,
> All day the fragrant cassia blossoms
> Bend toward me, delicate and subtle.

And in her poem "Dream, to the tune *The Honor of a Fisherman*," her vision grew profound and majestic. The political criticism in her "Poems Dedicated to Lord Han, the Minister of the Council of Defense, and Lord Hu, the Minister of the Board of Works" had been toned down and became implicit. But her love for the lost homeland was as strong as ever:

I send blood-stained tears to the mountains and rivers of
　home,
And sprinkle a cup of earth on East Mountain.

Here her tears were turned into a libation for the downfall of her family, her nation, and for the suffering of the people. The scope was sweeping, the pathos all-embracing. In her younger days, her tears were shed for her personal feelings of loneliness; for example, in the poem "A Song of Departure, to the tune *Butterflies Love Flowers*."

94

But now who will share with me
The joys of wine and poetry?
Tears streak my rouge.
My hairpins are too heavy.

The imagery of tears here successfully depicts the psychology of a resentful, sensitive woman in her loneliness. Ch'ing-chao is a master of employing imagery in diverse styles. She was the only Chinese woman author who mastered a great variety of styles and excelled in both the writing of *shih* and *tz'u* poetry.

Very little is recorded about her remaining years. She probably stayed with the family of her younger brother. She traveled to Chechiang Province when she was fifty-two, because of an alarm over an attack from the Tatars. She composed several poems there. When she was sixty-six, she visited Mi Yu-jen and showed him a calligraphy scroll written by Mi's father, the famous calligrapher Mi Fei. Apparently, old age did not diminish her devotion to art. She died some time after the age of sixty-eight.

LING CHUNG

NOTES

[1] The texts of our translations are based on *Li Ch'ing-chao Chi* (Shanghai: Chung Hua Shu Chu, 1962). We have translated in total sixty-seven poems, of which fifty are *tz'u* poems, seventeen are *shih*. All poems with a subtitle "To the tune . . ." are in *tz'u* form. The editors of *Li Ch'ing-chao Chi* express doubt on the authenticity of some *tz'u* poems. We have indicated these poems by a postscript, "attributed to Li Ch'ing-chao."

² See the biography of Li Ke-fei in *The History of Sung Dynasty* ("*Sung Shih*"). However, in *Chi Le P'ien*, written by Chuang Ch'o (fl. 1126), Ch'ing-chao's great grandfather is Wang Kuei, also a prime minister.

³ See *Chi Le Chi* by Ch'ao Pu-chih (1053–1110). Ch'ao was a good friend of Li Ke-fei. In Ch'ao's article "Yu Chu T'ang Chi" ("The House with Bamboos"), he described Li Ke-fei's residence in the capital.

⁴ See our translation: "Poems on Yüen Chieh's 'Ode to the Restoration of T'ang' to Rhyme with Chang Wen-ch'ien's Poem."

⁵ Li Ke-fei's friend Ch'ao Pu-chih often praised Li Ch'ing-chao's writings. See his *Feng Yüeh T'ang Shih Hua*.

⁶ *Li Ch'ing-chao Chi*, p. 71, excerpt from her "Postscript to *The Study of Bronze and Stone Inscriptions*."

⁷ See her poem "To the tune *Everlasting Joy*."

⁸ See the "Chronicle of the Life of Chao Ming-ch'eng and Li Ch'ing-chao," *Li Ch'ing-chao Chi*, p. 119. Chao T'ing-chih and Su Tung-p'o impeached each other in 1088. The basic materials of this biography are indebted to this chronicle.

⁹ Hu P'in-ch'ing, *Li Ch'ing-chao* (New York: Twayne Publishers, 1966), p. 33. Hu paraphrases passages from Ch'ing-chao's "The Postscript to *The Study of Bronze and Stone Inscriptions*."

¹⁰ See a source written by Ch'ing-chao's contemporary Chou Hui, *Ch'ing Po Tsa Chih*, chüan 8.

¹¹ Some articles and materials on this subject appear in *Li Ch'ing-chao Chi*, pp. 77–78, 154–55, 196–212, 238–52.

NOTES TO THE POEMS

Page 5, THOUGHTS FROM THE WOMEN'S QUARTER, to the tune *The Silk Washing Brook*. The "attributed" poems of Li Ch'ing-chao appear in some of the early editions of her poetry, but not in all. Scholars question the authenticity of them, especially when the persona of the poem is obviously a courtesan. It is unlikely that a woman with Li Ch'ing-chao's status and family background would write such a poem. This poem is an example: why should a wife try to make an assignation with her husband?

Page 6, to the tune *Picking Mulberries*. *Ling-hua ching* is either an octagonal bronze mirror or one ornamented with water flowers on the back. On the best highly polished bronze mirrors of the T'ang period, the ornament shows though like a faint ghost on the mirror surface.

Page 7, TWO SPRINGS, to the tune *Small Hills*. The original of "women's quarter" here is *ch'ang-men*, the Palace of Tall Gate, erected in the Han Dynasty. The queen of Emperor Wu lived in this palace in the second century B.C. Because she fell into the disfavor of the emperor, poet Ssu-ma Hsiang-ju wrote for her "the Rhyming Prose of the Tall Gate Palace," to describe her love for the Emperor and her loneliness. After the Emperor read the prose, he was so moved that he returned to her. This allusion might imply that Li's husband has gone to another woman, but now is coming back to her.

Tung-chün, Lord of the East, is the God of Spring, used as a metaphor for the man she loved. Here it is translated as "My lord has gone away to the East."

Page 10, WHEN THE PLUMS BY THE BACK PAVILION BLOOMED, to the tune *An Idle, Lovely Lady*. The last lines allude to a Tatar tune for the flute, very popular at Li's time, which was called "Plum Blossoms Are Falling"; so the music of the flute is often related to the falling plum blossoms, which symbolize the transiency of beauty.

Page 11, PEONIES, to the tune *I Celebrate the Clear Slow*

97

Dawn. The peony is regarded the queen of all flowers. They were carefully tended in the palaces through many dynasties. They symbolize the most favorite woman of the emperor.

The east side of the city alludes to Chia Ch'ang, who was brought up in the east side of Ch'ang An, the capital of the T'ang Dynasty. Chia became a favorite of Emperor Ming Huang, because of his skill in training fighting cocks. The southern streets of Ch'ang An were the courtesans' quarter.

The Brilliant Light Palace was built by Emperor Wu of the Han Dynasty. Night-bright pearls were inlaid on the walls, and the staircases were gilded; therefore, the palace was bright even on a dark night.

Page 13, CASSIA FLOWERS, to the tune *Partridge Sky*. "Partridge Sky" is a kind of cloud formation, called in English "mackerel and mares' tails," usually a sign of coming rains.

Page 14, NINTH DAY, NINTH MONTH, to the tune *Drunk with Flower Shadow*. Ninth Day, Ninth Month—a day of picnics on hills, chrysanthemum viewing, and outdoor love-making—was originally both a harvest festival and the autumn Feast of the Dead. The last lines of the poem allude to the famous line of T'ao Ch'ien: "I gather chrysanthemum flowers by the eastern hedge." This allusion adds a touch of the leisure and freedom of a Taoist hermitage to her poem. When her husband saw this poem, he composed fifty poems to the same tune. Then he mixed her poem with his and showed them to his friend Lu Te-fu. Lu pointed out that the best lines among these fifty-one poems were the last lines of her poem.

Page 15, THE BEAUTY OF WHITE CHRYSANTHEMUMS, to the tune *Beauties*. Yang Kuei-fei was the consort of Emperor Ming Huang, the most famous beauty in Chinese history. She was responsible for the revolt of An Lu-shan, which permanently crippled the dynasty. The Emperor fleeing from the capital was forced by his troops to order her hung to a pear tree. A *feng-huang* appeared and flew away with her blood-stained handkerchief.

Sun Shou (tenth century) was the wife of the warlord Liang Yi, famous for her coquetry.

In the third century, Han Shou was a minor officer in the office of Chia Ch'ung, the minister. The minister's daughter Chia Wu fell in love with Han Shou. He stole into her room and became her lover. The Emperor gave Chia Ch'ung some incense which was a gift from Nam Viet. Chia Wu stole it and gave it to her lover. The minister discovered their secret love by the scent of that incense in Han Shou's gown. He married his daughter to Han Shou.

Lady Hsü (sixth century) was a consort of Emperor Yüan of Liang. Her malicious trick infuriated the Emperor. Later when she was caught in an affair with an attendant she was forced to commit suicide.

Han kao may mean the bank of the Han River or may be an ancient name for the city of Han Kow.

Pan Chieh-yü was concubine of Emperor Ch'eng of Eastern Han. As the emperor's affection cooled, she presented him with a fan and a famous poem (translated in *The Orchid Boat*—"A Song of Grief") comparing herself to a summer fan discarded at the approach of autumn.

Page 19, REMORSE, to the tune *Rouged Lips*. "Every fiber of my soft heart" in Chinese is "every inch of my soft bowels." The bowels, as in earlier English and many other languages, were realistically considered the seat of disturbing emotion.

Page 20, to the tune *The Silk Washing Brook*. The *pi-han* bird is not the so-called Chinese phoenix *feng-huang* but a mythical gold bird that was sent to the emperor from Nam Viet, which spit gold. The last lines refer to the "candle flower," the red glowing wick of a burned-out candle.

Page 21, ON SPRING, to the tune *The Silk Washing Brook*. The jade zither *yao-ch'ing* was of course not made of jade but inlaid with it. It is the ancestor of the koto.

Page 22, SPRING IN THE WOMEN'S QUARTER, to the tune *Beautiful Nien Nu*. Nien Nu was a famous courtesan of early

T'ang, but the song is probably older, and she was named after it. For "the Day of Cold Food," see notes for next poem.

Page 23, THE DAY OF COLD FOOD, to the tune *The Silk Washing Brook*. "The Day of Cold Food," the day before the Spring Festival Clear Bright, *Ch'ing-ming*, is the Day of New Fire corresponding almost exactly to the Catholic rite of Holy Saturday. All fires are extinguished, a new fire is lit in the evening by flint and steel or bow drill, and all the fires in the community are started again from that fire. There is a long Confucianist euhemeristic legend with a typical Confucianist political content that Chieh Chih-t'ui, a noble hermit, refused office in the court of the Duke of Chin and hid in a forested mountain. The Duke set fire to the whole mountain, but Chieh preferred death to the government bureaucracy. This is an excellent example of the factitious Confucian interpretation of pan-Asiatic cult practices. In *The Book of Songs* ("*Shih Ching*"), the erotic poems of the Day of Cold Food are celebrated by different people who have preserved rites dating from the neolithic all over the world. Hannukah is an excellent example of a day of new fire which has received a political interpretation in Judaism.

Gathering wild flowers and herbs to play a game was a custom on the Dragon Boat Festival, the fifth day of the fifth month. The Day of Cold Food is in the third month. Li's line indicates that the people sensed the transiency of Spring and anticipated the customs.

The last line, which should read "Wet the swing in the garden," has always seemed to Rexroth so irrelevant as to be a corruption of the text. On the other hand swings in Chinese love poetry have an erotic significance, and apparently once had a family ritual connection with the Day of Cold Food.

Page 24, THOUGHTS FROM THE WOMEN'S QUARTER, to the tune *The Silk Washing Brook*. *Yi-hsi* could be interpreted in three ways. We have incorporated all three in this translation: 1) the leftover melon seeds, 2) the leftover wine in the cups made of rhinoceros horns, and 3) the golden tree. The golden tree of the South was another mythical tribute from Nam Viet, but to this day Chinese believe that sandalwood generates its own heat. The rhinoceros horn was believed to be one of the most potent aphrodisiacs.

Page 25, to the tune *The Bodhisattva's Headdress*. Chinese call the Milky Way the River of Heaven. The original text refers to the Dipper, the seven stars in Ursa Major.

Page 27, SORROW OF DEPARTURE, to the tune *Cutting a Flowering Plum Branch*. Orchid boats are floating pleasure houses. But, sometimes it is interpreted as the boat made of magnolia wood. This poem is packed with echoes. Wild goose is a cliché in Chinese poetry for "messenger" because they migrate every year regularly. Rexroth points out that "orchid boat" is also a common metaphor for the female sexual organ, as in this poem.

Page 28, FAREWELL LETTER TO MY SISTER SENT FROM AN INN AT LO CH'ANG, to the tune *Butterflies Love Flowers*. This poem was written in 1121, when Li was thirty-eight. She wrote it in a town called Lo Ch'ang, traveling on her way from Ch'ing Chou to Lai Chou, where her husband held the post of a magistrate.
"Sunlight on the Pass," or "The Sun Pass," was a famous song of departure. Sun Pass, Yang Kuan, is a town in today's Kansu Province, which was a passage from the Chinese frontier to the barbarian lands.
P'eng-lai are the mythical islands in the Eastern Seas where Taoist immortals reside.

Page 29, to the tune *You Move in Fragrance*. Golden flowers are the yellow chrysanthemum flowers.

Page 30, THOUGHTS FROM THE WOMEN'S QUARTER, to the tune *Nostalgia of the Flute on the Phoenix Terrace*. "Wu-ling Springs" alludes to T'ao Ch'ien's "Peach Blossom Spring." A fisherman discovered a utopian village in the mountains. Here Li alluded to her husband, who probably had taken a trip to the mountains.

Page 38, THE WU-T'UNG TREE, to the tune *Remembering the Girl of Ch'in*. The wu-t'ung tree, *sterenlia plalanifolia*, is said to be the only tree on which the so-called Chinese phoenix, the *feng-huang,* will perch, and it is the best wood for making musical instruments.

Between our lines 10 and 11 the Chinese text is corrupt.

Page 39, CASSIA FLOWERS, to a new version of *The Silk Washing Brook.* Yen Fu is the style name of Lo Kuang, a Taoist philosopher of the third century A.D. He was renowned as a most refined gentleman, eloquent, wise, modest, and also an excellent officer. General Wei Kuang praised him. "He is like a mirror which reflects the blue sky where all clouds are dispersed."

Page 39, BANANA TREES, to the tune *Picking Mulberries.* This poem must have been written after Li fled to the South in 1128, for banana trees grow only in South China, and also because she called herself *pei-jen,* a Northerner; hence, the translation of "this exile from the North."

Page 40, to the tune *Partridge Sky.* Chung Hsüan is the style name of Wang Ts'an, one of the seven leading poets of Ts'ao Ts'ao's time in the third century. Wang, a royalist of the declining Han court, fled from the capital after the warlords seized power. He went to Ching-chou to serve the Han prince Liu Piao, but the prince ignored Wang. Thus Wang wrote the rhyming prose, "Climbing the Tower," in which he lamented the downfall of Han, his homesickness, and his longing for the capital. Because of this allusion, Li's poem must have been written after she fled to the South.

Page 42, I GAVE A PARTY TO MY RELATIVES ON THE DAY OF PURIFICATION, to the tune *Butterflies Love Flowers.* The Day of Purification is the third day of the third month, when people held parties by rivers.

Ch'ang An, the capital of the T'ang Dynasty, alludes to the lost capital K'ai Feng. Hence, this poem must have been written after Li fled to the South.

Page 43, FADING PLUM BLOSSOMS, to the tune *Perfumed Garden.* Ho Sun was a poet who lived in the sixth century.

When he held an official post at Yang Chou, he very much enjoyed the plum blossoms in the garden of his office. Later he was promoted to a post in the North. He missed the plum blossoms so much that he asked to return to his former office in Yang Chou. His request was granted. When he came back, the plum tree burst into bloom, to welcome him. Compare the legend of the Japanese statesman Sugawara no Michizame (845–903), whose beloved plum tree followed him into exile, flying through the air to Kyushu.

Page 47, to the tune *The Perfumed Garden*. Li Ch'ing-chao in her *Postscript to the Studies of Bronze and Stone Inscriptions* describes how her husband and she would play memory games of the Chinese classics, and the winner would drink the tea. They grew so excited that the tea was usually spilled.

Page 49, SPRING ENDS, to the tune *Spring at Wu Ling*. Two Rivers, *shuang-hsi*, is in today's Chekiang Province; in 1135 when she was fifty-two years old, Li lived for a while in the nearby town Chin-hua. Her husband had died six years before, in 1129.

Page 51, ON PLUM BLOSSOMS. Li Ch'ing-chao wrote a subtitle for this poem: "Poets in the past always complained that to write about plum blossoms was very difficult, for you can hardly avoid vulgarism. Now that I have tried it, I totally agree with them." Li's poem is by no means vulgar. "Flute player" alludes to a legend in *Lieh Hsien Chuan*. Duke Mu of the State of Ch'in, in the seventh century B.C., had a beautiful daughter. She married a flute player, Hsiao Shih. One day, this couple rode on a phoenix and flew away from a jade tower (tower made of white marble). They had become immortals. "The flute player" in Li's poem must allude to her husband, who had died and was gone "beyond the sky."

Page 55, SENTIMENT. The title "kan-huai" is a mode of classical *shih* poetry. Literally "kan-huai" means "being moved to express personal sentiment and feelings." It is a very common title for *shih* poetry whenever a poet is writing about personal feelings.

At the end of the Han Dynasty in the latter part of the second century, warlords rose everywhere, among whom was Yüan Shu, whose style name was Kung-lu. Yüan Shu became powerful and later crowned himself. He soon began to fall because of his wasteful extravagance and could no longer support his own army. He went to the State of Ch'ing (today's Shantung Province) to depend on his relative Yüan T'an, another warlord. Ts'ao Ts'ao, in order to annihilate him, ordered Liu Pei to block his way. Yüan Shu was unable to reach the State of Ch'ing. When he was beseiged at Chiang T'ing, he sighed, "Is this where I meet my end?" He became seriously ill with his anger and weariness, and finally died.

Ch'ing-chou here must mean the State of Ch'ing, the general area of today's Shantung Province, not the county of Ch'ing where Li and her husband stayed for more than ten years in their country estate.

K'ung-fang hsiung, "the brother of the square hole," means coin, because a Chinese coin was round with a square hole in the middle. The reference is to pederasty, equated, as in Dante and Freud, with greed.

Mr. Wu-yu and Scholar Tzu-hsü are fictitious characters in Ssu-ma Hsiang-ju's rhyming prose *Tze-hsü Fu.* Ssu-ma Hsiang-ju (second century B.C.), the leading writer of his day, in this prose says Mr. Wu-yu (Mr. Nonexistence) was an envoy from the kingdom of Ch'u (of the Warring States) to the State of Ch'i. The King of Ch'i entertained him by taking him on a royal hunt. On his way back Mr. Nonexistence visited Scholar Tzu-hsü (Scholar No Such) and bragged that the hunt of King Ch'u, his own king, was far more extravagant and the landscape of Ch'u far more splendid than that of the kingdom of Ch'i. Ssu-ma Hsiang-ju uses these two fictitious characters to add an allegorical touch and as means to display his own gift in handling rich, decorative language in the form of rhyming prose.

Li Ch'ing-chao at the end of the poem says that she prefers to indulge herself in wild imagination of the past, and in a faraway splendid landscape together with Mr. Nonexistence and Scholar No Such, than to accept the company of local officials who care for nothing but amassing wealth.

This poem was written in 1121 when Li was thirty-eight years old. Li and her husband had lived in their country estate in the county of Ch'ing for more than ten years and enjoyed tremendously the life of hermits and scholars. In 1121 her husband was appointed as the magistrate of the county of Lai, his first official post after fourteen years of retirement. He went to his post first, and Li arrived there in the eighth month. She must have felt a strong sense of resistance to the life in a yamen, the compound which included both the office and dwelling of a magistrate.

Page 56, POEMS ON YUEN CHIEH'S "ODE TO THE RESTORATION OF T'ANG" TO RHYME WITH CHANG WEN-CH'IEN'S POEM, I. Yüan Chieh, a middle T'ang poet, wrote an ode in praise of Kuo Tzu-yi, the general who destroyed the rebellion of An Lu-shan. A monument was discovered when Li Ch'ing-chao was about seventeen. Many famous contemporary poets, including Chang Wen-ch'ien, a friend of her father, wrote poems on this discovery.

Line 1. *tien-sao*. This could mean fifty years of Emperor Ming Huang's glory passed away like a flash of lighting, or they fell asunder as though struck by lighting.

Line 4. Hsien Yang was the ancient capital of the Ch'in Empire. When Hsiang-yü entered the city in the third century B.C., he burned it down.

Lines 5-6. *wu-fang kung-feng*, "grooms of your five stables and kennels." In the T'ang Dynasty anyone with special skills in literature, art, or sports could be appointed *kung-feng*—special attendant in the court. Of the five attendants, four were for the hunting birds of falconry and one was for the hunting dogs.

Line 14. *ch'ing-cheng lou*, "Diligent Work Tower," was a several-storied building in the palace at Chang An, the T'ang capital, where the emperor often gave banquets and held audience.

Lines 18-19. The imperial concubine Yang Kuei-fei loved to eat lichees; a special horse relay was set up to deliver the fruit from Canton to Chang An, which is over a thousand miles. The horses were forced to travel fast so that the lichees would still be fresh when they arrived at the capital.

Line 21. Yao and Shun are legendary ancient sage kings, two of the culture heroes reputed to have founded civilization.

Line 26. Kuo Tzu-yi and Li Kuang-pi suppressed and defeated An Lu-shan's rebellion.

Line 30. By the lessons of the Hsia and Shang dynasties (twenty-first to sixteenth centuries B.C.) Li Ch'ing-chao means that the official histories say that the last emperors of these two dynasties were corrupted by concubines and ministers. In saying that Ming Huang fell into a similar trap, she reveals the strict Confucianism of the scholar-gentry. According to them, all dynasties fell from these causes—women, eunuchs, evil ministers, and foreigners. "When women rule, the land decays."

Last three lines. Chang Shuo was a powerful minister for three T'ang emperors; the last was Ming Huang, whom he helped to seize power when still a prince. Chang Shuo was very cunning, famous for plots, plans, and strategies, and he was probably one of the men most responsible for the glorious days of T'ang. But not long after Ming Huang succeeded to the throne, he was ousted by Yao Ts'ung, who told the emperor that Chang was plotting with the emperor's younger brother to seize power. Chang Shuo was exiled to a provincial post. Li in this poem says that the Emperor was blind to the feuds in the court and corrupted by Yang Kuei-fei, by his harem, and his foreign generals and advisors, and that everyone, even the Emperor, had to take the responsibility for the temporary fall of the capital. This is an unusual and courageous statement, for she was here alluding to a ruthless power struggle in the contemporary Sung court. The poem was written before she was twenty.

Page 57, II.

Line 8. Li Ch'ing-chao criticizes her contemporaries' poems on the monument because they did not present the whole picture of the rebellion, but merely extolled the achievements of the general Kuo Tzu-yi.

Line 10. The emperor not only doted on Yang Kuei-fei, but gave her three sisters titles of duchesses, as well as great wealth.

Line 15. An Lu-shan and Shih Ssu-ming were the leaders of the rebellion.

Lines 23-31. When the rebellion was repressed, Emperor Ming Huang returned (in 757 A.D.) from Szechwan to the capital, Ch'ang An. By then his son, Emperor Su, had succeeded to the throne. Ming Huang retired and lived in the Southern Palace.

At first, Emperor Su behaved as a most filial son; later, he listened to his minister Li Fu-kuo, who persuaded him that Ming Huang was conspiring to regain the throne. Li Fu-kuo rose to power through the influence of Su's wife, Empress Chang. In 760 A.D. Li forged an Imperial Decree requesting Ming Huang to visit the Western Palace, where from then on he was held under a kind of house arrest. His followers were all sent into exile. Kao Li-shih, the once powerful eunuch, was sent to Wu Shan.

Last two lines. When Kao Li-shih came to Wu Shan, he saw shepherd's-purse growing wild and wrote a poem:

In Ch'ang An they were sold by the peck.
Here near the five streams, nobody even cares to pick them.
One grows in the land of China, the other in that of the Tatars.
But they taste just the same.

Li Ch'ing-chao misses his irony and attacks Kao Li-shih for caring only about the trivia of cheap vegetables in his exile, instead of attacking Li Fu-kuo and Empress Chang. She is unjust to Kao, a politician with conscience who was loyal to Ming Huang, in contrast to Li Fu-kuo and the all-powerful eunuchs of late T'ang and Ming dynasties.

Shepherd's-purse (*Capsella bursa pastoris*) is a crucifer, a member of the mustard and cabbage family. It is circumpolar, grows on wasteland, and is an escape from imported fodder in the Southern Hemisphere. In the nineteenth century, it was still sold as a vegetable in American markets, and Robert Fortune in *His Wanderings in China* says, "Besides the more common vegetables, shepherd's-purse and a species of clover crowd the markets and are used by the natives; and really these things, when properly cooked, are not bad." It is an antiscorbutic and a mild diuretic.

Page 59, POEMS DEDICATED TO LORD HAN, THE MINISTER OF THE COUNCIL OF DEFENSE, AND LORD HU, THE MINISTER OF THE BOARD OF WORKS. These two poems were written in 1133, seven years after Emperor Hui and Emperor Ch'in were captured and brought to the North by the Chin Tatars. The present Emperor Kao was the son of Emperor Hui and the younger brother of Emperor Ch'in. Emperor Kao established a court in the South. Many historians agree that the main purpose of Emperor Kao's envoys was not to ask the Chins to release the two captured emperors, but to beg for a truce. In fact, they think Emperor Kao felt threatened that the two emperors might be released, because once released, they would become claimants to his throne. Lord Hu and Lord Han's mission was by no means easy, because during 1127 to 1133, many envoys had been sent to the Chins. Most of those envoys were tortured and imprisoned. None ever returned. However, since in 1132 and 1133 the Sung army had won several battles, they were in a better bargaining position. Han and Hu came back safely and brought back an envoy from the Chins to further negotiate the treaty. Of course they did not bring back the two captive emperors. The first poem was a parody on the court audience. Subtle sarcasm runs through the poem. For example, it is utterly disgraceful for an emperor ever to say openly, "I am willing to give up land," no matter for what reason. The second poem is more outspoken in voicing Li Ch'ing-chao's opposition to the Sung court's begging for a truce.

The title. The Minister of the Council of Defense is the highest official in charge of military policy and decrees. Lord Han, Han Hsiao-chou, was a great-grandson of Han Ch'i, a prime minister and scholar and the patron of Li Ch'ing-chao's father and grandfather. *Ping-pu,* Board of War, was a mistake. It should be *kung-pu,* Board of Works, for Lord Hu, Hu Sung-nien, had never held a post in the Board of War. The Minister of the Board of Works was in charge of public property, official seals, coinage of money, and natural resources.

The subtitle. *Liang-kung* literally means "two palaces." One refers to the emperors in exile—Emperor Hui and his son Emperor Ch'in—as well as most of the royal family, all held by the Chins in the remote North. The other palace is Emperor Kao's, who finally set up his court in 1132 at Lin An (today's Hang Chou).

Page 59, I. To Lord Han.

Line 1. This is the third reign year of Shao-hsing (1133). Emperor Kao had succeeded to the throne starting from 1127, and had already reigned for seven years.

Line 7. Yüan Yü-ch'ing was a very virtuous man in the T'ang Dynasty. A friend praised him, "It is said that a most virtuous man would appear every five hundred years. You are qualified to be one of them." Thus, Yüan changed his name to Yüan Pan-ch'ien, Yüan the half a thousand.

Line 8. *Yang-chiu. Yang* is the hot element; *chiu,* nine, is the largest of the digits. *Yang* and *chiu* put together mean the extreme blazing period, the perilous time, 1129 to 1132, when Emperor Kao's court fled all through South China, pursued by the Chins.

Line 9. The monument was erected in 89 A.D. at Yen Jan Mountain in Mongolia when, in the Han Dynasty, the Chinese general Tou Hsien defeated the Huns.

Line 10. *Chin-ch'eng liu* literally means "the willows of the Golden City." The city is in today's Kansu Province. In the first century B.C., General Chao Ch'ung-kuo defeated the Hsi Ch'iang Barbarians, started an agricultural military colony there, and planted willows along the roads.

Line 12. Literally, "the worry of frost and dew," meaning the longing for parents. Nurture of children is compared to dew which waters the grass.

Line 13. In *Tso Chuan,* when the Duke gave food to Yin K'ao-shu, Yin did not drink the meat soup. The Duke asked for the reason. Yin said, "My mother has tasted whatever I have eaten in the past, but has not yet tasted this meat soup. Could my lord send this soup to her?"

Line 22. Han Yü (768–824), a famous statesman, writer, and Confucian scholar of the T'ang Dynasty.

Line 26. Kao and K'uei were two renowned ministers in the legendary age of the sage King Shun. Kao was Minister of Justice, K'uei was Minister of Ceremony.

Line 27. Wang Shang was a court official and relative of Emperor Yüan of the Han Dynasty in the first century B.C. His appearance was stern and awesome. A Hun chief who came to pay tribute to the court was so terrified by him that he fled China after the audience.

Line 28. Tzu-yi, Kuo Tzu-yi, was the general who subjugated the Turkish An Lu-shan rebellion in the eighth century.

Line 39. Paste was used to seal up the envelope. The purple color could only be used by the Emperor, for purple and gold were the imperial colors.

Last two lines. When the Chinese sign a treaty, they use, instead of ink, blood of a dog and a horse to pledge their oath.

Page 66, II. To Lord Hu.

Line 3. Many tales in Chinese history tell of an Emperor or general who won over the hearts of his soldiers when he took off his own robe and gave it to a soldier on a cold day. That was one of the reasons, the stories say, why the soldiers fought to the death for him.

Line 4. In the third century B.C. the Prince of the State of Yen sent a bravo, Ching K'o, to assassinate the Emperor of Ch'in, who was devouring one by one the independent states. It was a very difficult task. At the farewell party by the River Yi, Ching K'o sang to the Prince and his friends: "The wind blows *hsiao hsiao*. Cold is the water of River Yi. The brave man is going away. He will never return."

Line 13. During the Spring and Autumn Period (8th to 5th Centuries B.C.), the generals from the State of Sung and those from the State of Ch'u held a peace conference. The generals from Ch'u wore weapons inside their robes, intending to ambush the Sung generals.

Lines 14–15. In the middle of the eighth century, the Turkish rebellion shook the kingdom of T'ang. In the latter part of the eighth century, during the reign of Emperor Te of T'ang, a Turkish general came to the T'ang court and requested the Emperor to consider a peace conference. However, the Turkish prime minister requested the Chinese Emperor to change the locale for the conference from P'ing Liang to Yüan Chou. The Emperor turned down this suggestion for fear the Turks would ambush the Chinese army in the mountains of Yüan Chou.

Line 16. K'uei Ch'iu is in today's Honan Province. In the seventh century B.C., Duke Huan of the State of Ch'i invited dukes from many states to attend a conference for an alliance against the Northern Barbarians, the Huns, the Hsiung-nu, at this place. Chien T'u is also in today's Honan Province. In the seventh century B.C., Duke Wen of Chin invited many dukes to hold a conference for an alliance there, after he defeated the army of the Southern State of Ch'u and erected a palace at Chien T'u.

Line 18. During the northern expedition of General Huan Wen in the fourth century, when he won the decisive battle, he ordered his secretary Yüan Hung to write a eulogy. Yüan Hung was a talented writer. Without dismounting his horse, Yüan immediately completed seven pages of a beautifully written eulogy of victory.

Line 19. In the fourth century B.C., Prince Meng-ch'ang from the state of Ch'i loved to patronize talented people from all walks of life. Once he was imprisoned by King Chao of Ch'in, who intended to kill him. Eventually the prince escaped from the prison and rode with his followers to the Yao Han Pass, a gate in the Great Wall. They reached the pass at midnight, but the gates were closed as the guards would only open them when the cocks crowed. One of the Prince's followers mimicked a cock's crow so well that the cocks for miles around all echoed him. The guards believed it was dawn, opened the gate, and let them through.

Line 22. The pearl of Sui and the jade disk of Master Ho are poetic synonyms for priceless treasure. In the Chou Dynasty (eleventh to eighth centuries B.C.), the Duke of Sui saw a wounded serpent. He applied an herb to its wound and cured it. Later, the serpent found a great pearl in the river and presented it to the Duke. In the eighth century B.C., Master Ho from the State of Ch'u found an uncut jade rock. He presented it to the King. However the king's jade cutter said there was no jade in the rock. The King angrily accused Master Ho of swindling him and cut off his left foot. When the King died, Master Ho brought the rock to the new King. The same thing happened: he lost his right foot. When this king died, the old Master Ho embraced the rock at the foot of Ch'u Mountain and wept for three days and nights. The young King sent a messenger to ask him for the reason of his lamentation. Master Ho said, "I am not lamenting the loss of my feet, but because a rare jade is discarded as a rock, and a man of integrity is accused of being a swindler." The King sent his jade cutter to work on the rock. Indeed there was a huge piece of excellent jade inside. The King named the priceless work of art made from it the "jade disk of Master Ho."

Line 30. Chi Hsia was a town in today's Shantung Province. According to *The Book of History* (*"Shih Chi"*), in the Warring States scholars flourished in the State of Ch'i. By the city gate of Chi Hsia, the scholars used to hold fervent discussions on the affairs of state and the problems of men.

Line 38. "The peach trees" allude to a poem by Yüan Chen of the ninth century, called "Verse on the Palace of Everlasting Prosperity." The poem starts with a description of the unattended palace after the Turkish An Lu-shan rebellion:

The Palace of Everlasting Prosperity is overgrown with bamboos.
No one attends them, they crowd in throngs.
The thousand-leaves-peach-trees cover the walls.
When the wind blows, petals fall like red rain.

Page 65, A SATIRE ON THE LORDS WHO CROSSED THE YANGTSE IN FLIGHT FROM THE CHIN TROOPS. Hsiang Yü (third century B.C.) became the ruler of all the Chinese States when he seized the capital and the last Emperor of the Ch'in Dynasty. Four years later in 202 B.C., this young hero was cornered against the River Wu by Liu Pang, and committed suicide because he was ashamed to escape. Liu Pang became the first Emperor of the Han Dynasty. Here Li Ch'ing-chao implies her sharp criticism of the Sung court, which fled to the South of Yangstze River.

Page 66, ON HISTORY. The Han Dynasty lasted for four hundred and twenty-five years, from 206 B.C.–219 A.D. The continuity of the dynasty was interrupted for fourteen years by Wang Mang from 9 to 23 A.D., who crowned himself and changed the dynastic title to Hsin. Hence, the Han Dynasty was divided into the Former Han and the Latter Han. Chi K'ang was a famous writer in the third century. Historians believe that he was executed by Ssu-ma Chao, because of his satire on Ssu-ma's usurpation of the Wei Dynasty. In the satire, Chi Kang compared Ssu-ma to the founders of the Shang and Chou Dynasties, who in turn had overthrown the previous kings. According to Confucius, these founders are sage kings. But Chi K'ang condemned them as traitors, for they rebelled against and killed their own kings. Li's quatrain is very intricate and condensed. In twenty Chinese characters she discusses four historical events: 1) the succession of the Shang Dynasty to the Hsia Dynasty, 2) the succession of the Chou Dynasty to the Shang Dynasty, 3) the succession of the Hsin Dynasty to the Han Dynasty, and 4) the succession of the Chin Dynasty to the Wei Dynasty. However, at the bottom of this poem she is satirizing a contemporary event. After the Sung Court fled to the South in 1126, the barbarian Chins in 1129 appointed a puppet government at K'ai-feng, with Chang Pang-ch'ang as the puppet king. Hence, the "excrescence" in her poem alludes to the Dynasty Ch'u headed by Chang Pang-ch'ang.

Page 67, WRITTEN ON CLIMBING EIGHT POEMS TOWER. This poem was written in 1134 when Li was fifty-one and lived at Chin Hua Town in Chekiang Province. Shen Yüeh is a poet and literary critic of the fifth century. He was appointed as the prefect of this area. A tower was built west of Chin Hua under his supervision. When it was completed, he wrote eight poems to celebrate its beauty. Thus, the tower was later named the Eight Poems Tower. It is situated at the meeting place where Chin Hua River and Wu Yi River flow into one, which in turn is connected with many far-reaching waterways.

In the Southern Sung Dynasty, the district of Liang-che Lu (approximately in today's Chekiang Province) was divided into fourteen counties.

Page 67, OUR BOAT STARTS AT NIGHT FROM THE BEACH OF YEN KUANG. Yen Kuang (first century A.D.) was a friend of the prince who became Emperor Kuang Wu of the Han Dynasty. When he ascended the throne, the Emperor offered his old friend power, fame, and wealth, but Yen declined and stayed by Che River as a fisherman and farmer. The beach of Yen was named after him.

Page 68, IN THE EMPEROR'S CHAMBER. This is a *t'ieh-tze*, a poem written for a party given by the emperor on a festival.

The following four poems were written on the fifth day of the fifth month, the festival of poets in commemoration of Ch'ü Yüan, the poet who drowned himself in the fourth century B.C. They were written in 1143 when Li was sixty years old and lived in Lin An, the capital of Southern Sung. In the Sung Dynasty, wives of high officials were granted titles by the emperor. They could also present poems to the throne at the festival parties. One of Li Ch'ing-chao's relatives was a lady with a title. Li wrote these four poems on her behalf.

A Taoist legend says that when the immortals Lao Tzu and Chang Tao-ling visited Szechwan, a jade couch with twisted carved legs emerged from the ground. Lao Tzu sat on it and preached. When Lao Tzu and Chang departed after his preaching, the couch sank into the earth. Only a hole was left in the ground.

In the last two lines, Li advises the Emperor that it is better to contemplate the affairs of the state in the light of the torches than to enjoy parties and entertainments in the fragrance of the incense. To burn incense was a custom at festivals to expel evil spirits.

Page 68, To THE EMPRESS. The rearing of the silkworms occurs in the fourth lunar month, and since this poem was written on the fifth day of the fifth month, it was already completed in the imperial garment workshop. According to an ancient Chinese ritual which had been practised by many dynasties, the Empress is the chief attendant of silkworms in the whole nation, just as the Emperor, as a model for the kingdom, plows a field in early spring. According to The Book of Rites of the Chou Dynasty ("Chou Li"), the second term for rearing silkworms, supposed to be in the fifth month, was forbidden, because it was the period to breed horses. The spirit of silk worms and that of horses are believed to have the same origin and therefore their breeding should not be overlapped. This belief probably derived from an ancient folktale about the origin of the silkworm. A daughter pledged that whoever brought back her father could take her as wife. A horse from their stable then mysteriously disappeared. A few days later, the horse brought back her father. Her father was so angry at the horse that he killed it and dried the horse-hide on a tree. The hide suddenly flew to the girl, enveloped her, and soared to a mulberry tree. With the girl wrapped in the hide like a silkworm in a cocoon, they were transformed into silkworms.

The Emperor Kao had no sons then. His son died very young. Thus, he and the empress had no heir.

Page 69, To an Imperial Lady. Three palaces were residences for the empress and chief consorts. Noon was the highlight of the festival of the fifth day of the fifth month. Dumplings wrapped in leaves would be eaten then. Women decorated their hair with herbs and flowers, and at noon they would take off these decorations. That was why in the poem they made up their faces before dawn.

Page 70, To the Imperial Concubine. The Chinese title is *Kuei Fei Ke*, "Noble Consort's Chamber." This title is given to the first-ranking Imperial Concubine, next only to the Queen, like the consort of the great T'ang Emperor Ming Huang, Yang Kuei Fei, the most famous of all Chinese beauties. All the talks about the Emperor Kao's begetting a son and many sons were futile; because the Emperor did not have an heir, the throne was succeeded by his remote nephew after he died. The stewardesses of the harem who kept records of the Emperor's sex life gave his concubines different bracelets. The one who was to sleep with the Emperor that night wore a silver bracelet on her left arm; after intercourse she wore it on her right. If she became pregnant she wore a gold bracelet. The subject of Li's poem was pregnant. Kou Yi is the name of the palace of the Han Dynasty where the concubine of the Emperor Wu lived. She was called Kou Yi, which means "hook." The legend says she held her fists clenched tight since she was born. When the Emperor summoned her to his bed, the first time he touched her, her fingers opened. Kou Yi's son succeeded to the throne. Li implies that the subject of her poem may have given birth to the heir apparent. Unfortunately, she in fact later gave birth to a daughter.

Chao Yang Palace, the Bright Sun Palace, was the residence

of the Empress, and Li compares the Imperial Concubine to the Empress herself.

"Cypress seed bed curtains" might have actually been made of juniper berries to perfume the bed, or they might have been made of blue pearls that looked like juniper berries. The character for seeds/berries also means sons. It is a pun.

Page 73, DREAM, to the tune *The Honor of a Fisherman*. There is no other poem like this written by a woman in Chinese literature. It is a poem of mystical trance directly descended from the *Li Sao* ("Encountering Sorrow") of Ch'ü Yüan of the fourth century B.C., the shamanist poems *Ch'u Tz'u* ("Songs of the South," translated by David Hawkes), and the mystical, Taoist, alchemical writing of Ko Hung of the Three Kingdoms. Illustrations taken originally from a treatise of Ko Hung can be found, misinterpreted, in Carl Jung's *Secret of the Golden Flower*, and in Leo Weiger's *History of the Religious and Philosophical Opinions of China*, fifty-second lesson. Chinese Taoists adopted cosmic visions of this kind, often induced by eating the sacred mushroom.

"The huge roc bird," a favorite Taoist legendary creature, can be equated with what we now know to be the autonomic nervous system; the little boat with the Serpent Power, hidden in the perineal plexus, and the Immortal Islands in the East with the thousand-petaled lotus of Indian Yoga. Rexroth thinks that the three mountains in the Eastern Sea in poems like this and the *Songs of the South*, interpreted in terms of erotic mysticism, were very fashionable in the more sophisticated intellectual circles, especially in Shanghai, during Kuo Min Tang rule. The secret key was considered to be the sixth chapter of the *Tao Te Ch'ing*. This poem raises the question: How many of Ching-Chao's "love poems" are, like those of Hafiz or Dante, actually mystical?

Page 74, WRITTEN ON THE SEVENTH DAY OF THE SEVENTH MONTH, to the Tune *You Move in Fragrance*. This poem was written on the Seventh Day of the Seventh Month, a festival for lovers. The Cowboy and the Weaving Girl are the two stars on the opposite sides of the Milky Way, Altair and Vega. According to Chinese folklore, after the Cowboy and the Weaving Girl got married, they loved each other so much that they ignored their duties completely. The Emperor of Heaven became so angry at them that he separated them by the River of Heaven, the Milky Way. Later the Emperor was moved by their love and permitted them to meet each other once a year on the Seventh Day of the Seventh Month. He ordered the magpies to form a bridge for the Weaving Girl to cross the River of Heaven.

According to *Po-wu Chih,* written by Chang Hua in the third century, in a folktale the ocean to the east of China is connected to the River of Heaven. In autumn when the water floods, people who live by the ocean could sail to heaven on a raft.

Page 75, A MORNING DREAM. According to the *Book of History, Shih Chi,* and other sources, An Ch'ing-sheng was the pupil of the Old Man on the River. An Ch'ing-sheng used to sell medicine by the sea. The local people called him the Man One Thousand Years Old. When the first Emperor of Ch'in traveled to the East in the third century B.C., he talked to An Ch'ing-sheng for three days and nights, and believed he was a Taoist immortal. Later the Emperor sent many messengers to the Eastern Sea to look for him. Their ships returned empty-handed because of the storms. In the second century B.C., Li Shao-chün, a court officer, told Emperor Wu of the Han Dynasty that when he traveled on the ocean, he saw An Ch'ing-sheng riding on the waves and eating dates as huge as gourds. O Lu-hua was reputed to be an immortal in the Chin Dynasty. In A.D. 360 she descended to the house of Yang Ch'üan and taught him the Taoist secret of immortality.

According to Taoist beliefs, the immortals used to ride on huge lotus flowers. Their diameters were about one hundred feet. These flowers bloom on the peaks of T'ai Hua Mountain. They are called Jade Well Lotus, and their roots are as huge as boats.

Page 81, AT A POETRY PARTY I AM GIVEN THE RHYME CHIH. Hsiang Ssu was a poet of the ninth century. He lived as a hermit in the mountains for thirty years. Yang Ching-chih, a high officer in the court, admired Hsiang's poetry very much, and praised his poetry to everyone he met.

Page 81, to the tune *Immortals on the River Bank*. The poem was written in the spring of 1128 when Li fled to the South and arrived at Nanking, where her husband held the post of the city magistrate (like the mayor today). "To light the lantern" means to light it for the lantern festival on the fifteenth of the first month. As the first lady of the city, she was supposed to lead the ladies to light lanterns of a great variety of designs and shapes.

In the preface of this poem, Li indicates that the first line was directly quoted from an early Sung poet, Ou-yang Hsiu. However, Li's poem is superior to Ou-yang's in depth, pathos, and a sense of passing time.

Page 82, to the tune *Everlasting Joy*. The capital of Northern Sung was in Pien, the K'ai Feng City. Defeated by the Chins, the Sung moved the capital south to present-day Hang Chou. Presumably Li wrote this poem in Hang Chou, recalling days in the lost capital. The Feast of Lights (lanterns) occurred on the fifteenth of the first month, when people competed with beautiful lanterns and showed off their clothing and ornaments, gifts of the New Year.